Illumination in the Flatwoods

ILLUMINATION IN THE FLATWOODS

A Season Living Among the Wild Turkey

JOE HUTTO

DRAWINGS BY THE AUTHOR

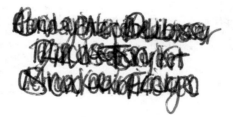

THE LYONS PRESS
Guilford, Connecticut
An imprint of Globe Pequot Press

Lyons Press is an imprint of Globe Pequot Press

10 9 8 7 6 5 4

Printed in the United States of America

ISBN-13: 978-1-59921-197-8

Library of Congress has previously cataloged an earlier edition.

ACKNOWLEDGMENTS

Many people have offered support, both moral and technical, throughout this project, and I would like to extend my gratitude.

The Florida Game and Fresh Water Fish Commission was particularly gracious in allowing me to go forth with this experiment. Robert M. Brantly, Frank Montalbano, L. Ross Morrell, and David Cobb were all especially generous and helpful in this process.

For reading manuscripts and offering technical advice I am indebted to James J. Miller, Helge Swanson, Janisse Ray, Rebecca Chalker, Victoria Mathews, Kathy McCord, Stanley J. Olsen, Robert K. Godfrey, Joe Funderburk, David W. Steadman, and Bill Harrell. Their support has been immeasurable.

To my patient editor, Lilly Golden, for her expertise and guidance, I will always be thankful. Her sensitivity for the subject matter has made a potentially difficult phase of this book a pleasure.

I am extremely grateful to my wife, Claudia Zahuranec. Without her loving counsel and indulgence this project would have been impossible.

For typing and computer services, Janet Tudor was indispensable in helping to decipher and organize my stacks of field notes and journals.

A special note of thanks is in order to Lovett E. Williams, Jr., whose research, technical advice, and encouragement were instrumental in the completion of this book.

HEAD ANATOMY OF ADULT WILD TURKEY GOBBLER

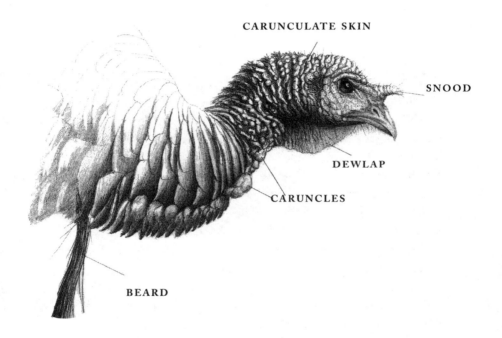

CARUNCULATE SKIN

SNOOD

DEWLAP

CARUNCLES

BEARD

Upper Surface of the Left Wing of the Wild Turkey

ALULA OR WINGLET

PRIMARY COVERTS   GREATER SECONDARY COVERTS

SCAPULARS

PRIMARIES

TERTIALS

SECONDARIES

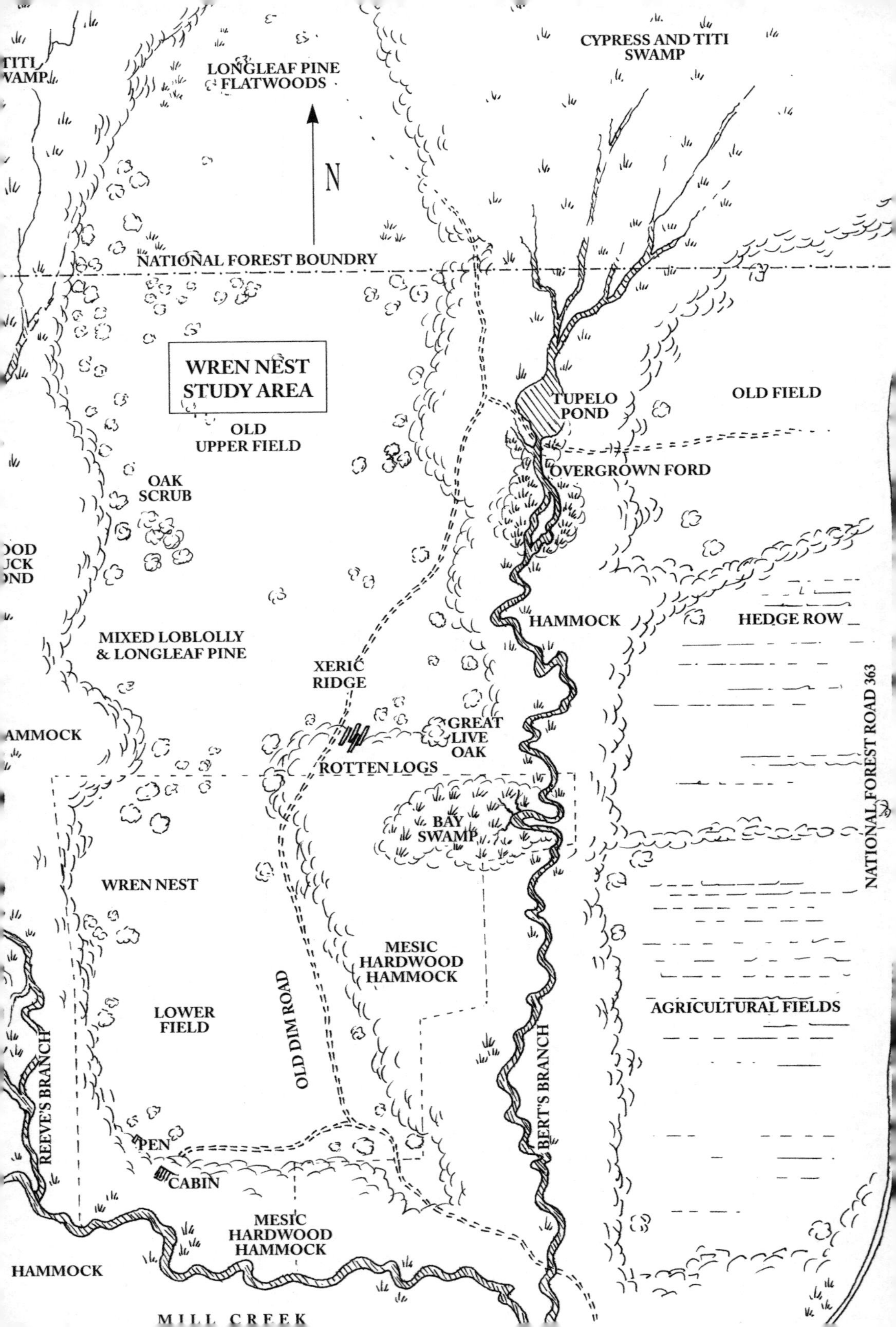

CYPRESS AND TITI SWAMP

TITI SWAMP

LONGLEAF PINE FLATWOODS

N

NATIONAL FOREST BOUNDRY

WREN NEST STUDY AREA

OLD UPPER FIELD

OAK SCRUB

OOD UCK OND

MIXED LOBLOLLY & LONGLEAF PINE

XERIC RIDGE

AMMOCK

ROTTEN LOGS

GREAT LIVE OAK

TUPELO POND

OLD FIELD

OVERGROWN FORD

HAMMOCK

HEDGE ROW

NATIONAL FOREST ROAD 363

BAY SWAMP

WREN NEST

MESIC HARDWOOD HAMMOCK

AGRICULTURAL FIELDS

LOWER FIELD

OLD DIM ROAD

BERT'S BRANCH

REEVE'S BRANCH

PEN

CABIN

MESIC HARDWOOD HAMMOCK

HAMMOCK

MILL CREEK

INTRODUCTION

The wild turkey has the distinction of being the only species in North America identified by name as wild. Perhaps, in part, the name serves to appropriately distinguish the wild from the domestic variety, but surely it also denotes the wild turkey's most conspicuous characteristic—that it is profoundly inconspicuous. Frequently, I encounter people who have never observed a wild turkey even though they live in an area where these birds are considered to be abundant. Only in recent years, with the development of portable radio-telemetry technology, has wild turkey behavior begun to come to light. These studies are, of course, limited in their scope and provide only broad overviews of behavior—as revealing as the use of aerial photography would be to observe human behavior. We could identify traffic and road systems, settlement patterns, and places of specific activity, but we would observe little of the day-to-day, minute-to-minute nuances of individual behavior and personality. Having remained intrigued with these birds and a little frustrated with their elusiveness for much of my lifetime, I chose to use the mechanism of "imprinting" as a possible window into the secret life of the wild turkey.

Imprinting is the phenomenon that serves the newborn of most socially organized animals in immediately identifying his parent and to some degree his species. In certain highly socialized species of birds, called "precocial," that are born alert and fully ambulatory, such as ducks, geese, swans, and all gallinaceous birds, including pheasants, quail, partridge, grouse, chickens, and turkeys, imprinting occurs rapidly at birth and in most cases is unalterable.

Although I have had various experiences with imprinting as a tool to gain entry into the lives of many different species, and even though all that I do predisposes me for such activities, what is contained in the following account was completely unforeseen. Had I known what was in store—the difficult nature of the study and the time I was about to invest—I would have been hard pressed to justify such an intense involvement. But, fortunately, I naively allowed myself to blunder into a two-year commitment that was at once exhausting, often over-whelming, enlightening, and one of the most inspiring and satisfying experiences of my life.

I have scratched through Pleistocene bone beds tens of thousands of years old, and lifted out the fossil bones of wild turkeys that once shared a very different landscape with a multitude of strange creatures that did not endure.

I have analyzed skeletal remains of wild turkeys deposited in caves by native American hunters in the desert Southwest and wondered how our lives could be so intertwined for so many thousands of years and yet they remain complete strangers to us.

Examining every bone, identifying each articular surface, separat-ing every muscle group, counting seeds, berries, insect parts, and bro-ken glass contained in crops and stomachs, I wandered through the labyrinthine anatomy and physiology of dead wild turkeys and yet I knew nothing—they remained mysterious.

In archives and libraries I pored over monographs, research papers, and books, but still I knew more about the contents of wild turkey stomachs and the parasitic inhabitants of their intestines than about their behavior—their nature.

For hundreds of hours I sat concealed in camouflaged blinds, fogging my binoculars, listening to the soft whir of audio- and videotape, and alternately releasing the shutter and rewinding my still camera. But wild turkeys are not sedentary creatures, and I was rarely permitted to observe one for more than five minutes—more often our encounters could be measured in seconds.

As a wildlife artist I have attempted to render them, calling on my experience, my research, and my many videotapes and photographs to help me portray the nobility in their eyes and posture, but was I able to express anything that is the truth about the wild turkey? I was never sure.

In this study and through my unusual relationship with these birds, I was allowed passage into their world and their experience. They provided a conduit of sorts, but one that would allow only the most buoyant elements of my being to cross over. A fragile bridge that would support neither a scientist nor an artist. Not camera, pen, or the smallest slip of paper was allowed passage. And so, eventually, leaving these things scattered behind me, I found myself at times experiencing a very different reality and the gift of glimpsing, if only momentarily, the world through another's eyes.

The most dangerous pitfall for ethologists, observers of animal behavior, is the employment of the anthropomorphic analogy—attaching human attributes to animal behavior. It is only by analogy, however, that we have any hope of gaining real insight into the lives of other creatures. All biological organisms to some degree have similarities. The old anthropocentric notion that human beings somehow are distinctly removed from the rest of the animal kingdom was a poorly conceived vessel that will no longer float. If we are careful not to assign particularly human qualities to other species, then it is not inappropriate to identify our similarities and gain insight in this way. It is critical for the observer to maintain a position that affords a broad horizon, one that attempts to explain behavior in a light that is brighter than our own immediate experience. It is an exercise in overcoming our intellectual presumptions and, probably most important, our condescending human arrogance. Whether attempting to achieve understanding of an exotic culture or an unfamiliar species, a position of superiority is always a recipe for failure.

Nietzsche once said, "Convictions are more dangerous enemies of truth than lies." Every scientist knows the danger of doing research with the intent or need to validate a favorite hypothesis. The more impassioned a researcher is toward making himself right, the more likely he is to find a way to verify incorrectly that hypothesis. It is a gaping hole into which scientific careers often fall. Like the aspiring archaeologist who on his first summer field experience is desperate to make some profound discovery—some real sense out of the dirt: Suddenly, after two post holes are uncovered fifty feet apart, he closes one eye, squints, looks from one post mold to the next, and pedantically exclaims for all to hear: "My God, these two post holes are in a perfectly straight line!"

Similarly, love for one's subject matter has often been the undoing of good science. I hope the reader will allow me a certain latitude, as I confess that my data must surely, in this way, be askew. This is, after all, my personal journal, and so I hope I may be forgiven as I wander into the realms of wonder, sentiment, humor, and even, on occasion, the irresistible anthropomorphic metaphor. I hope these liberties are sufficiently tempered with sound, objective, unbiased observation.

I do not wish to represent this writing as scientific research on wild turkeys. It is not. That is the respected province of a few dedicated wildlife biologists to whom I am indebted. Their research has afforded me a solid foundation of data from which to begin. Although I consider this experience to be more an expression of passion or a love affair of sorts, I do believe that I have made observations that will be of interest to many students of natural history.

Ultimately, this study is not about science but about a way of looking—of looking at an old world, through our old perceptions and attitudes, with new eyes.

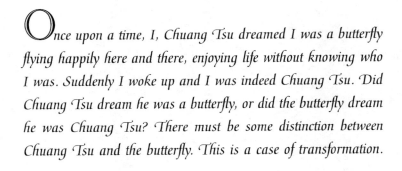

Once upon a time, I, Chuang Tsu dreamed I was a butterfly flying happily here and there, enjoying life without knowing who I was. Suddenly I woke up and I was indeed Chuang Tsu. Did Chuang Tsu dream he was a butterfly, or did the butterfly dream he was Chuang Tsu? There must be some distinction between Chuang Tsu and the butterfly. This is a case of transformation.

—Chuang Tsu
fourth century B.C.

PART I

As I stare at the eggs before me, I try to perceive the potential that is contained within each one. It strikes me that an egg is a most remarkable phenomenon, so commonplace, so familiar, and yet sublime. Pleasing to look at and sensual to hold, it is one of those perfect creations of nature that is disarmingly simple from one point of view and staggeringly complex from another. Even the chicken egg, refrigerated and sterile, reminds us of something precious as we cradle it carefully in our hands.

A living egg, with its warmth, its purity, and its sleeping potential, is a wonder. Who has not had the experience of peering down on the nest of a bird and being shocked by the sight of this uncanny perfection contrasted with the rough fabric of the nest?

An egg is a mechanical device used to transport and protect a living embryo. It is an architectural exercise in the conservation of space and in structural integrity. It is a vehicle for traveling down the fallopian tube and eventually out into the cold hard world, and a vehicle for traversing time—a time machine that can reconcile twenty million years in only twenty-eight days.

There is a wonderful principle in evolutionary biology known as Haeckel's biogenetic law that is stated simply: Ontogeny recapitulates phylogeny. That is, every organism must retrace its evolutionary development from a one-celled organism to its contemporary manifestation as it develops from fertilization to birth. Although an oversimplification, this concept has valid applications. As an embryo develops, it begins with simple mitosis—one cell dividing into two. There is then a predictable progression through stages, each of which represents a rung on the phylogenetic ladder. A fetal pig will pass through successive developmental stages whereby it will share features with and be scarcely discernible from the fish, the amphibian, the reptile, up the evolutionary path to a stage representing its primitive mammalian ancestry. Only then will it begin to find its particular biological identity as a pig. Up to that point it is bound to revisit each ancestral stage of its development.

This principle, of course, holds us biologically accountable, as well. Evolutionary development is a process of building on existing attributes, not of starting from scratch. Every structure in our body from our skeleton to our DNA serves as testimony to this principle. We are a walking paleontological repository. This is why the skeleton of a frog laid next to that of a man, with the exception of size is bone for bone very much the same—a quantitative difference only. We are a frog run amock. We have to biologically retrace our steps through antiquity every time one of us is conceived.

These particular eggs that lie before me now represent something very important to me. Each harbors a mystery, something untamed and virtually unknown to us—an embodiment of wildness. They are the wild turkey.

The eggs are smooth, of a dark bone color, sprinkled uniformly with very small flecks of sepia, and slightly larger than a chicken egg. They are carefully laid in orderly rows on brown towels that hold them off of the screen that forms the bottom of racks within a well-made wooden incubator. The temperature in the incubator is a precise 99.5 degrees F. The wet bulb thermometer indicates that the humidity is exactly 85 percent. A fan gently blowing across a pan of water in the top of the incubator ensures that the humidity will remain constant and the air will not become stale. Eggs must breathe and so are very vulnerable to gases that could accumulate in the closed incubator if the air were not allowed to circulate. Turkey eggs, I am told, have a very narrow range of tolerance for both temperature, which must remain within one degree of the recommended 99.5 degrees F., and humidity, which must remain very close to 85 percent. The incubator must be monitored constantly for any variation.

The only light is from an empty brooder that I have fashioned from a plywood box and a drafting table lamp that I normally use in my work. The narrow storage room in which I sit has no windows and a concrete floor. It is a relatively cool night, but I am cozy as I sit on a folding camouflage stool peering through the window of the incubator. The room also contains a few of my tools, a washer and dryer hookup but no washer or dryer, a hot water heater that hisses periodically, duffel bags stuffed with camping gear, and duffel bags stuffed with photo blinds. Oddly, there are three rubber turkey decoys in a row on a shelf. They seem to be staring at the desiccated toad that sits exactly where he must have died long before I moved into this old house over a year ago. He is not particularly attractive but provides an atmosphere of continuity. I worry that if these eggs do not hatch soon, I may be found in a similar condition by the next occupants of the house.

I am anxious about this project, but I also have a very good feeling about what could become of this if we have any luck at all. It all began about ten days ago with the chance acquisition of these eggs, but it is clear that all this really began many years ago, and in some ways it seems I have always dreamed of trying this experiment.

I remember an incident that occurred when I was twelve years old. My eyes burn from getting only a few hours of sleep. I am slightly nauseated from eating a greasy breakfast at 4:00 A.M. Sitting alone in an inky, damp darkness, I am pulled by nagging feelings of anticipation and fear. Propped against a tree I cannot see, in a forest totally unknown to me, I can hear my heart beating loudly as I consider the possibilities that the sunrise may hold. I have doubts: I may do the wrong thing, make the wrong move, disappoint my father and his friends, or be forever lost in this dark forest. I am alone in some deep North Florida forest, an hour's drive through the night in a direction I have never been, deposited here by my father in the chilly morning darkness of early March. There is a forest of contingencies also, and my mind swims hopelessly lost in this thick blackness that envelops me. I fear that I am not ready for all of this and regret having nagged and pleaded, hoped and prayed to be here. For me this is very important. This is not sitting next to my father in a duck boat. This is not a late afternoon cornfield with my father watching me from a nearby pecan tree. This is me alone in a big forest, by myself in the dark with a loaded shotgun across my lap. I have listened carefully, I have studied, I have imagined every scenario my mind will permit. As my father's footsteps disappeared into the darkness, I tried to review everything I need to remember.

Gradually, I begin to see the dim silhouette of limbs against the sky. I see that I am in a mature forest of very large trees whose leaves have not returned from the winter. A faint illumination softens the mantle of blackness that has covered me. Birds begin making scolding noises that seem to express regret at having their blanket of darkness rolled back.

At last I can see myself and am reassured that I exist beyond the limits of my apprehensions. The suffocating blackness is replaced by a strange presence. I can feel it as it presses against me and accompanies the cool air into my eyes and chest. Shivering slightly, I see my camouflage clothing, but this vaporous presence makes me feel uncovered and vulnerable as it saturates me. My eyes water, and my face becomes tight as I squint through the predawn mist.

The sky begins to glow slightly in the east. The sun must be rising. I remain in a viscous soup of undifferentiated blues and grays, as the first signs of real color begin to appear across the sky. A wash of cool air moves across my face as though flushed from its hold on the forest floor. It moves into the trees briefly as if the world has been startled into taking its first breath.

More birds begin to peep and chatter around me. I am consoled by the familiar voice of a cardinal. Spring peepers, which I also recognize, begin a chorus below me. The forest slowly awakens with life. A crow sounds in the distance. Startled, I wonder how so much life and energy could have remained so well hidden around me.

I try to remember what my purpose is here. I am supposed to try to lure a wary and elusive inhabitant of this forest to me without allowing myself to be seen. I feel clumsy and conspicuous. I strain to see through this mist that hides the base of the more distant trees. My father assured me that the creature lives in this very wood, and I try to imagine what he would look like slowly moving through this area. I struggle to hear. I think I understand what he should sound like, but I do not really know. A kaleidoscope of sound reverberates around me. A woodpecker pounds a hollow tree in the distance, and briefly I wonder if that could be the sound, but I know it is not.

A golden glow bathes the uppermost limbs of the tallest trees. Another pulse of air stirs and pulls a shiver from somewhere deep inside me. I try to remain motionless. I know the rules. I remember what I have been told.

I remember my turkey caller. Quietly, I remove it from my pocket. My hands are clumsy from the chill, but the cedar wood and slate of the caller feel familiar and reassuring. As with a musical instrument, I have practiced and rehearsed, and this is my debut. I nervously scrawl out faint white circles on the thin slab of slate framed in my palm. I am startled by the sound it produces. It cuts through the air like a rude sharp stick. Exposed and embarrassed, I put away the yelper and try to be inconspicuous. I strain to perceive some sort of acknowledgment but hear only a squirrel jump to the ground and run a short distance. Eventually my courage returns, and I retrieve my caller and try once more. Again I am shocked by the unpleasantness of the sound and how foolish it makes me feel. I replace the caller in my coat pocket knowing well that any wary creature within a mile has surely been frightened away.

The forest quiets. The excitement of dawn has settled into an alert stillness. I press my back into the tree in an effort to become a part of it.

I hear something walking some distance directly behind me. Judging by the sound, it must be very large. It seems to be coming toward me, rapidly at first and then more slowly as it nears. My heart quickens. It could be a fox or even a deer. I want to turn and look, but I know to remain motionless. As this woodland prowler draws near, its pace slows and I can hear individual footsteps in the dry leaves of the forest floor. It has weight as it sinks through the mulch; small twigs give way and snap. As I become aware of the heavy, slow, and deliberate cadence of two feet, it occurs to me that I am being approached by a person. The person seems to be carefully stalking—another turkey hunter must be here. Instinctively, I remain still, afraid to identify myself to this stranger. I wonder if it could be my father searching for me even though he left in the opposite direction. But surely he would not return so soon. The person very slowly walks up behind me, perhaps only twenty feet away, and stands still. I can feel his eyes on the tree that separates us. I can feel his ears as he listens for the sound of my heart beating. I am certain that he knows I am here. It must be my father, but I am afraid to move. A very long time seems to pass without a sound, and I begin to wonder if the person could have walked away without my knowing. I start to slowly turn my head and strain my eyes to see peripherally, but I am afraid to look. Then another movement in the leaves, and he moves one step closer. He definitely knows that I am here. It is as though *I* am being stalked. Suddenly, I am surrounded by a wondrous sound that seems to originate from the earth itself. I am enveloped by a single resonating pulse from some enormous drum that I can feel within. It is more of a pressure in my chest than a sound in my ears. I absorb its ascending vibration like a sponge. Overcome with the knowledge that the stranger that produced this remarkable sound could not be human, I am paralyzed as this creature seems to observe me through the tree. I feel his inquiry—his consciousness—on the back of my neck. Behind me is a profound presence, something powerful and apprehensive like the cocked hammer of a gun. He takes a couple of short, careful steps and once again becomes motionless, looming only a few feet behind me. When eventually he takes several more cautious steps, I realize that he is moving away. He stops several times, and I can sense his scrutiny. Then his footsteps disappear slowly into the forest. My breath returns. Something has been drawn from me, and I am left very cold.

I never saw that great bird on that cool spring morning, but he inadvertently shared something important with me, and I would never be the same. A wild turkey had changed my life.

In the spring of 1991 I lived with my wife, Claudia, on a historic North Florida plantation. It was established in the 1830s with corn and cotton, but its focus shifted in the early 1900s from agriculture to recreation. When people ask what is grown there today, the answer is simply quail. Unlike most businesses (and this place is very busy) the overhead far exceeds the income. Such places are allowed to exist at the pleasure of their owners, and the pleasure of these owners is quail. Quail provide the foundation for what is a significant industry, employing many people, a small army of employees, most of whom live on or near the plantation and often serve generation after generation. With its laundries, rifle and skeet ranges, stables for horses, stables for mules, sheds for wagons, sheds for tractors, homes for owners, homes for managers, homes for employees, pens for dogs—lots of dogs—road graders, bulldozers, huge standing water tanks, and, of course, guns, a quail plantation is a little like a military base with a good attitude. When the commanding officers show up in the fall for hunting season, the place suddenly looks ready for inspection, with fresh white paint everywhere, grounds well manicured, and everyone very busy— all for quail. A manager told me that one of the owners divided the number of quail killed each year into the overhead and determined that the quail cost $9,000 per bird.

One portion of the plantation, a portion that includes five or six thousand acres and thus constitutes one of the smaller parcels, had historically had fewer "birds" than the other parcels to the north. So the order came down through the chain of command that this parcel was deficient in "birds" and so must be "improved," meaning that the quail "carrying capacity" of the land should be increased. This was attempted in two ways: by harvesting a significant percentage of mature native pine and by eliminating the hardwood transition areas between the high rolling pine land and the wet bottoms, ponds, and creeks. The latter was accomplished by shoving down the offending hardwoods and burning them in piles. This operation took a couple of years, and as young hardwoods began coming up in these recently cut-over areas, the plantation staff began an intense mowing operation, so that the indigenous seed-bearing plants that are more beneficial to quail would prosper. Small feed plots of corn and various millets were also planted in the spring throughout the woods and fields. In addition, very large fields were planted, maintained, and harvested annually, the grain stored in silos and fed out gradually all year in quail feeders through-out the plantation.

As all of this mowing and agricultural activity was going on, one day I overheard one of the tractor drivers complain about the daily inadvertent destruction of wild turkey nests by the mowers. Thinking it would be interesting to try to imprint and raise a couple of wild turkeys, I mentioned to him that I would be interested in getting some eggs if he destroyed another nest. I imagined incubating four to six eggs, of which two or three might survive. Also, the thought of wild turkey eggs rotting on the ground or being eaten by predators was abhorrent. I couldn't help but wonder about the hundreds of quail nests that were also being destroyed, and whether there wasn't a bet-ter season in which to improve the quail habitat.

The following evening, May 2, I returned from town to find a large, stainless-steel dog bowl full of wild turkey eggs waiting on my steps. The truth is, I had not really believed I would get any eggs and was utterly unprepared. The eggs felt only slightly warm to my touch, suggesting that they were being incubated by the hen when the nest was destroyed, but were cooling fast.

Frantically, I tried to think of what to do. I had no incubator—not even a heating pad. I put the bowl of eggs on top of the hot water heater, which felt warm, hoping it was not hot enough to kill the eggs. I then covered the bowl with towels, sprinkling some water on the bottom towel to provide some humidity. Considering that the eggs must have been already stressed from becoming cool, I now feared the possibility of overheating them. Remembering a friend two counties away who had raised turkeys from eggs, I headed out into the night in search of a suitable incubator. Luck prevailed. My friend Bill Harrell not only had a very good incubator but also offered me immediate advice on the dos and don'ts of turkey egg incubation.

In addition to the temperature, moisture, and atmospheric conditions required by turkey eggs, there are other considerations that must be rigorously observed: A mark must be made on each egg to use as a reference, so that the eggs may be properly turned at least twice each day. Failure to turn the eggs will result in the yolk settling and eventually sticking to the bottom, ultimately causing the death of the embryo. This would have been straightforward enough except that after the twenty-fifth day, turning must stop, so that the young bird may have time to position himself on his back, which is necessary for the "pipping" and hatching process. ("Pipping" is the pecking of the first small hole in the eggshell prior to actual hatching.) This requires one to know the precise day that incubation begins, and of course I did not.

I returned home to the waiting eggs after midnight and immediately set up the incubator in the storage room that adjoins my house at the end of a small carport. The heater heated and the fan fanned. I lined the screen racks and the bottom of the incubator with terrycloth towels. Young turkeys, or poults, will develop a condition, referred to by my friend as "spraddle leg," if the newly hatched turkey comes into contact with any smooth surface that allows his feet to slip under him. The tendons on the insides of the legs become permanently stretched, causing the legs to be turned outward; the turkey can never stand and must be destroyed. This condition can occur within a matter of minutes, and the birds are at risk for up to several days following hatching.

I rushed to prepare the eggs for the waiting incubator. First I had to "candle" the eggs. By observing eggs in front of a strong light it is possible to make a rough determination of their stage of development. Eggs that are infertile appear translucent compared to developing eggs. Judging by the well-defined, dark shapes within these eggs, I concluded that they were well developed, with only one of the sixteen being infertile. In order to preserve the sterile egg, I later made small holes at each end and blew out the contents, which were quite fresh. Statistically, this represented a very large clutch of wild turkey eggs, a typical clutch consisting of twelve or thirteen.

With a black marker I made a small dot on each egg and placed them carefully in rows on the middle rack with all the dots facing up. This final step was not accomplished until after 1:00 A.M., so the eggs had been without proper incubation for at least seven hours. I could only hope that some might survive. While incubating, wild turkey hens do not generally leave their nest, or "recess," for more than an hour and a half, especially in the cooler evening hours or at night, according to researchers Lovett Williams and David Austin.

The following day I began turning the eggs and periodically turning off the fan and talking to the eggs—first looking carefully around to make certain that no one was in the area; I did not want to be caught talking to eggs. Actually, it has been documented by Lovett Williams that for a considerable time prior to hatching, the young turkeys are well developed within the eggs and make vocalizations that are audible to the hen. The hen also makes faint utterances that possibly serve to imprint the developing poults to her voice. The Austrian animal behaviorist Konrad Lorenz, who did pioneering work on the mechanism of imprinting, made note of similar vocal behavior among nesting graylag geese. As a boy, I stumbled upon the imprinting phenomenon while attempting to raise various wild animals. (For years, it was more or less my mission in life to collect as much newborn wildlife as possible.)

It has been my experience with other birds and animals that if imprinting is not accomplished carefully, it may be only fragmentary and incomplete, making communication confusing or impossible.

Once while in college, I held a job on a deer ranch working with wildlife biologist Matt Wisenhunt. As an aside, we ordered some day-old game farm turkeys to accompany some other barnyard birds that we had, including chickens and pheasants. The turkeys were raised in a commercial poultry brooder and provided with food and water. The young poults were allowed to wander about the barnyard and would follow us about as we did our chores. We were much too busy for any direct interaction with them, and this resulted in the turkeys becoming partially imprinted on our feet. One ridiculous consequence of this was a sexual fixation by the mature gobblers on shoes. (Any shoe left unattended in their vicinity would gain their undivided attention, and obligatory courtship behavior would culminate in futile efforts to mate.) Interestingly, these same turkeys, having been raised in a flock, also imprinted on each other and therefore displayed normal sexual behavior between gobblers and hens.

Since imprinting in birds and other animals occurs generally during and shortly after birth, and in the case of the wild turkey, even possibly prior to hatching, I resolved to do whatever was necessary to accomplish this as thoroughly as possible. Everything I have read and all the experience I have had indicate that young wild turkeys are very difficult to manage. Therefore, I suspected that the effort and time I invested then would tend to ensure some measure of success in the project down the road. And so secretly, in both Wild Turkey and English, I began to putt, yelp, purr, and offer soft words of encouragement, hoping to let the tiny occupants of the eggs know that when they were ready, someone would be waiting.

May 4, Saturday

It has been two days since the eggs arrived. This morning, as I open the incubator to turn the eggs, I notice a faint septic smell. After smelling each egg individually, I find one to be dead. Perhaps it died as a result of being stressed prior to incubation. In any case, I fear for the rest.

I open the dead egg and find that it contains a small wild turkey in its latter stages of development. I estimate that growth is a week to ten days from being complete and calculate that I must stop turning the eggs in a very few days. Fourteen eggs remain.

May 7, Tuesday

I return from town this afternoon to find another bowl of wild turkey eggs waiting on my doorstep. Some are stained with blood, and I gently sponge these off so that they will not be prevented from "breathing." I place the fourteen new eggs on a separate rack within the incubator, without candling, and designate them in my journal as clutch #2. Later, the tractor driver tells me that the hen had been killed on the nest by the mower and at least one egg was broken. Apparently, there was a well-formed young turkey in the broken egg, since the driver reported seeing some movement. These eggs are obviously well developed, so I should stop turning them shortly after beginning incubation (6:00 P.M.). I immediately start vocalizing to the eggs and will increase the frequency of these conversations from several times a day to every hour or two. For the first time, I feel that someone in an egg might be listening. I fear for clutch #1. They seem quiet and inert in comparison to clutch #2, which somehow makes the entire house, even from a distance, appear gravid and expectant.

I have been told that when rearing domestic turkeys it is customary to have newborn chickens available to teach the newborn turkeys, by example, how to peck. Presumably, young turkeys are not clever enough to accomplish this by themselves. I grudgingly obtain two Rhode Island Reds from the feed store just in case, but I find this whole notion insulting. I also buy a small waterer and fifty pounds of commercial turkey "starter" feed. I think fifty pounds of feed optimistic, but the man at the feed store assures me that if I hatch even a few young turkeys, this large bag will disappear very fast. The feed companies are so impressed with the turkey's ability to eat that they do not package a smaller quantity.

May 10, Friday

At 5:00 P.M. I enter the incubator for conversation and notice a small hole in the upper surface of one egg in clutch #2. A small hole, the size of a pinhead, but on close examination I see the movement of what appears to be the tip of a tiny wild turkey bill. I turn off the fan in the incubator, and as I talk to the eggs, I can hear faint peeps coming not only from the pipped egg but distinctly from others as well. In fact, as I speak softly and make soft yelping sounds, a small chorus of peeping wells up from the eggs, and then slowly dies down, as if they have grown tired. I close the incubator and restart the fan. For the first time I believe that there are actually wild turkeys in these eggs.

Eventually the pipped egg becomes active again. Three hours have passed since I first noticed the activity in this egg. I turn off the fan and begin talking and making light yelping noises. The little turkey responds with peeping and attacks the eggshell with a bite on the shell and a movement of the head that he repeats in the same way over and over again. Gradually, a uniform line begins to develop that seems to be confined to a particular latitude, approximately one-third of the way from the larger end of the egg. The hatching activity is punctuated with rest periods lasting only a minute or two. Often, it seems that he resumes hatching in response to my vocalizations. At last, the end of the egg falls away, hinged by only a small piece of membrane. The little turkey pushes at the door he has created and scrambles free of the egg. The entire process has taken fifty-five minutes.

This new arrival struggles awkwardly with his newfound freedom. He is wet, and gravity seems to be pulling in every direction while an untested equilibrium attempts to establish the correct placement of head and feet. For a moment the little wild turkey lies motionless and helpless, striving to catch his breath. I remember to make a sound. Speaking very softly, just above a whisper, I make a feeble attempt to console him in what seems to be a desperate and confusing moment. Instantly, he raises his shaking wet head and looks me square in the eyes. In that brief moment I see a sudden and unmistakable flash of recognition in the little bird. Something completely unambiguous transpires in our gaze, and I am certain that the young turkey absolutely knows who I am. I am totally disarmed as the little creature struggles across the towel, never interrupting his gaze, and eventually presses himself against my face, which awaits him at the edge of the shelf. Gradually, he makes himself comfortable, his peeps and trills subside, and I realize that something has also moved inside of me.

As the new arrival sleeps, I quietly close the incubator door and contemplate a gravity that now tests my own equilibrium. I sit silently next to the incubator and am lulled by the gentle hum of the fan. Occasionally in life, as we flow along, we are presented with ideas or opportunities that alter our lives immediately and dramatically—the resumption of an academic career, a sudden change in occupation, the pursuit of some lurking artistic interest, or a consuming love affair. Unexpectedly, something presents itself that we know is exactly the thing to do at that particular moment, and so we are willing to pay the price of setting all other interests and commitments aside. It is an instant priority that superimposes itself over all other things. This is one of those times in my life. Inadvertently, I have been afforded an opportunity and a responsibility that will for some unforeseen time profoundly alter my life. I have had a chance encounter with these little birds and for us it is love at first sight.

I check my new little companion, who sleeps peacefully, before turning in for the night. Two more eggs have pipped. There is no hatching activity, so I close the incubator and turn out the light on the brooder. If more hatching occurs in the night, an imprinting opportunity won't be missed as long as the incubator remains completely dark.

But entering the house, I realize that I cannot miss any of this, and so I set my alarm to check on the eggs periodically through the night. One more egg pips; all else remains quiet.

May 11, Saturday

At dawn I awaken spontaneously, quickly dress, and rush to the incubator. Three more young turkeys are hatching. Two are completely free of the egg, and one is wrestling with a stubborn hinge. The first arrival from the night before is very fluffy in comparison to his new siblings and has joined the hatching activity in the back recesses of the shelf. When he sees my face, he stumbles and hops along until he reaches me. There is considerable peeping and activity in the incubator as the latest arrivals try to become oriented. I speak softly and make light turkeylike yelps and purrs. Within a matter of minutes the three newcomers awkwardly join us by the edge of the shelf. I cover the four with my hand and hold them close to my face, and eventually the trills and peeps subside as they fall fast asleep. I remove the empty shells from the incubator and notice that more eggs are pipped and one is starting to hatch. Since drying time on hatchlings is six to eight hours, I will begin putting the little ones in the brooder this afternoon.

Once the actual hatching begins, it is a very physical process, with small turkeys and eggs rolling all about. It is impossible to keep the eggs properly oriented, so I check each egg and make sure that if it has a pip hole, the hole is turned to the top. Clutch #1 is very quiet, radiating a silence that makes me uncomfortable. I worry about their welfare not only within the eggs but also because if they are hatched much later than clutch #2, they will be smaller and weaker and thus bullied by the older clutch. If they hatch a week apart, it could be a month before the two clutches could be safely put together. This could make things logistically complicated.

I pass more time being close to the new arrivals, but it is clear that they are not at all confused about my identity. When the incubator is closed, the newly hatched turkeys are calm and comfortable in the warm darkness. They stay together in a downy pile and sleep peacefully.

At 1:00 P.M. poult #5 falls free of his egg and flounders briefly around on the soft towels. Like the others he does a double take when I speak. Making immediate eye contact with me, the little turkey pushes and stumbles until he reaches my face. The eyes seem to be very important in this process. It appears to be with great relief that the turkeys see and identify my eyes as belonging to my voice. Invariably, after locating me and the others, they seem to discharge the apprehension of hatching and are left only exhausted. They all then fall into a peaceful sleep attended by more or less continuous faint peeps and trills. Poults #6, 7, and 8 follow shortly after #5.

Around 5:00 P.M. small turkey #9 makes his appearance. He has difficulty breaking free of the shell, so I intervene without his knowledge, and he eventually joins me in much the same manner as the others.

Many newborn birds are not attractive to our eyes and are appreciated mainly by their parents. Gallinaceous birds, however—chickens, quail, pheasants, and turkeys, to name a few—are to the human eye irresistibly cute. Newborn turkeys are very round and are covered with a thick, soft down, broken up into patterns of dark brown distributed over a field of dull yellow. Their bills are pale in color and are capped by the little protuberance called the egg tooth, which assists in the hatching process and is shed in a day or two. The legs and feet are a light brownish pink. The eyes are dark brown, almost black, and very intense. The brown markings on their heads are well defined, intricately arranged around a dorsal stripe, and each bird's markings appear to be unique.

The first real wild turkey behavior that I observe in the incubator is pecking. Anything that is small and contrasts with its surroundings is identified as a curiosity, presumably edible, and is aggressively pecked. The Rhode Island Reds are out the door. I will find them a good home, while wild turkeys everywhere stand vindicated and these will not have to suffer the indignity of receiving tutorials from domestic poultry. Newborn wild turkeys will peck and eat before they can stand.

I transfer several of the older and dryer hatchlings, who by now are becoming restless in the incubator, to the brooder, a plywood box (twenty-four by twenty-four inches wide and eighteen inches high) with no top. It is lined with a light brown towel and provided with a feeder, a waterer, and a drafting table lamp, which hangs over one corner and down into the box. The lamp is equipped with a 100-watt bulb and generates considerable heat. Spring nights and mornings can still be quite cool here, and the young poults are immediately drawn to the warmth.

I feel that this is a critical time in the imprinting process, so I remain as close as possible to the turkeys in the brooder and try to continuously interact with them. They are left alone only for seconds as I retrieve an apple or cola. All heads rise briefly as I crunch into my apple. They are very alert to my eyes, so I keep my face close to them, let them become comfortable with my hands, and maintain a regular dialogue of appropriate turkey noise as well as my natural voice. I do everything I can to make them unafraid of being handled, as I am sure that as time passes the necessity to handle them and pick them up will be ongoing. They must not dread being touched. I notice that they are uncomfortable with anything that passes over them, an apparent innate response to the possibility of aerial predators. I frequently pass my hand back and forth over them, and in a short time they begin to ignore it. I will reinforce this many times, not to interfere with their innate wariness of danger from above, but to disassociate that danger from my hand.

I check on the incubator and find that the young arrivals there are doing well and seem glad to see me. None of the four remaining eggs in clutch #2 is pipped, but I suddenly notice, on the shelf below, an egg with a distinct little hole. As I look more carefully, I am amazed to see that many of the eggs in clutch #1 are pipped though none is actively hatching as of yet.

It is difficult to account for the phenomenon of synchronized hatching that often occurs in large clutches of eggs. M.A. Vince, in his 1969 study, reports large quail nests, which can have as many as twenty-four eggs, completing the entire hatching process in less than two hours. The survival advantages accompanying a short hatching time are obvious, but the precise mechanisms that trigger the hatch are not well understood. It has been suggested that the vocalizations and activity made by the emerging young, as well as those still in the process, stimulate the clutch into simultaneous hatching. It may be that the activity of clutch #2 is inspiring clutch #1 to hatch. In any case, I am delighted that there are little turkeys in clutch #1, and this will make life easier for all of us.

I spend most of the night waiting for some further activity in the incubator, but all remains quiet. I place the remaining hatchlings in the brooder, and all are well with one exception. One little turkey is weak and listless. The oldest are becoming strong and active.

May 12, Sunday

I awake at dawn and rush to the incubator, but no hatching activity has occurred. Almost all of the eggs in clutch #1 are pipped, but the remaining four eggs in clutch #2 appear to be dormant. The young poults in the brooder, who were sleeping in a large pile, are awakened by my presence and become very active and vocal. I am saddened to find that the poor one has died in the night. He must have had some congenital problem. All of the others seem strong and enthusiastic. They are eating well and have begun to use the waterer. With the poults actively exploring the brooder and seemingly eager to interact with me, I spend much of the day on a cushion next to the busy group. I keep my face and hands close to the little turkeys, who seem to enjoy being in direct proximity to me. None seems to mind being picked up and held, and they will actually be comforted to the point of falling asleep in my cupped hand. They respond immediately and directly to my voice with peeps and trills, and if I continue talking or softly yelping, they come across the brooder and make intense eye contact with me. When I stop, they resume normal behavior.

Small flying insects are attracted to the brooder light in sufficient quantity to keep the turkeys continuously involved in chasing them about. They attack the insects aggressively, but their strikes frequently miss their marks. The slightly larger insects are captured and shaken until dead and then eaten. Behaviors indicating a sense of possession and jealousy are already in evidence. A poult will protect a captured insect as others chase after the prize.

Although they are not proficient, the poults already spend time attempting to preen their down and trying to adjust tiny flight feathers, which are only slightly developed at the time of hatching. These flight feathers are visibly more developed in the individuals that are the oldest by only hours. Young wild turkeys can fly well in seven days.

As the day progresses, I worry about clutch #1, which has pipped but is not hatching. Perhaps it was too early for them to hatch, but they were forced into pipping by the hatching activity of clutch #2. I also worry that they are finding it impossible to break away their shells for some reason, perhaps because of humidity or some other technical problem that was accentuated by being in the incubator for a longer period of time. Perhaps I should intervene and attempt to help them out of the eggs. I choose to do nothing, trusting their ability to know when to begin.

I see movement around the pip holes, some of which are slightly enlarged. When I speak softly to the eggs or make a faint yelp, they respond with muffled little turkey chatter. We are all ready. As of around midnight, all is quiet; there is no activity, but all seem well.

Assuming now that the remaining four eggs in clutch #2 are either sterile or dead, I observe that the hatching process took exactly twenty-four hours. This would be consistent with a normal hatching time, as W.R. Healy reports a variation of between twelve hours and forty-eight hours in the hatching of wild turkey eggs in incubators.

May 13, Monday

When I check the incubator at daylight, hatching is underway in clutch #1. By 9:00 A.M. three have hatched, and more are in the process. I remain with the incubator, imprinting the new arrivals and encouraging those in transit. Since the brooder is at my side, it is possible to interact with the older ones as well. The hatchlings in the brooder are strong and active, and I think it is about time for their first adventure into their real world.

The morning warms up nicely, and the day is very sunny. I pick up the entire brooder and carry it outside. The little turkeys show interest and concern about this sensation but not fright. As I cradle the brooder across my chest, my head is directly over the little ones, who watch and listen carefully as I carry them outside. I sit down beside the brooder on the grass in the backyard. The young poults are impressed with the great, bright blue opening that reaches out over them, and with erect posture observe this blue phenomenon carefully. Quickly their behavior returns to normal, and I begin picking them up, one by one, and placing them on the ground in a small corral formed by my legs. Immediately, they begin exploring and pecking around in a world that is obviously more interesting than the brooder. They busily feed and do not, as I thought they might, seem confused or run for cover. Slowly, I experiment by letting a few out of the corral, and I am pleased to find that they are very businesslike and simply begin foraging through the grass and leaves. I have no way of knowing if they are sufficiently imprinted to stay by my side or respond to my call. A few individuals begin to wander and explore fifteen or twenty feet away, but soon I notice that they seem to be on an invisible tether and after a brief adventure away, run short of confidence and come running back. They are responsive to both my voice and my yelping, which direct them to my side. I also make a high-pitched purr—an "alarm purr," known to be a component of the wild turkey hen's vocabulary—which brings everyone running to my side in a panic and hiding around my folded legs. This behavior was immediate, unanimous, and manifested itself fully upon my first initiation of the call. I am relieved to discover this and will be careful how and when I reinforce this behavior.

It is amusing to see these small wild turkeys try to scratch in the dirt and leaf mulch. They know what to do but lack the strength and dexterity to do it well and often fall over in their attempts. I also notice that as one little turkey is approached by another, the approached turkey responds by strutting, a behavior normally associated with adult gobblers. He drops his wings, tucks back his head, and raises his little nub of a tail.

They find much to eat in the grass and leaves and are frequently in aggressive pursuit of small insects. But after an hour or so they become tired and are inspired by the warm sun to sleep in a pile around my folded legs. I gather up the sleepy turkeys, and we return to the storage room and the busy incubator.

More little poults are coming, and I spend a very pleasant hour or two greeting new arrivals. Such an urgency and desperation accompany their arrival that I worry about not being present at the moment of hatching. I imagine them wandering hopelessly around the incubator, terrified, disturbing the unhatched eggs. So far, I have managed to be present at every hatch, however, and they are quickly consoled with a little contact and conversation. The trust that they bestow on me at that moment fills me with a great sense of responsibility. Each time one of these little birds comes into the world and identifies me as the object of his complete devotion, I find that I am deeply moved. They are so small and vulnerable, but they represent to me something rare and extraordinary, even powerful. I am very respectful of them.

As of 2:30 P.M. there are seven new poults and more on the way. I return the older ones to the backyard for more foraging and notice that they are more vigorous than this morning. We browse for an hour or so and then return to the incubator in the storage room.

By 6:30 P.M. there are ten new poults in the incubator. The remaining eggs in clutch #1 have pipped, but the four eggs from clutch #2 still have not shown any signs of life. Surely they are sterile.

After returning from our outing, I notice that one of the poults from clutch #2 is acting peculiar. He is having obvious difficulty with his equilibrium and is periodically making jerking movements. Since his symptoms occurred suddenly, I wonder if he has eaten something toxic. So that he does not get chilled or bullied, I place the weakened poult in the incubator.

Several of the poults in the incubator are dry and becoming rest-less. I worry about mixing the two clutches, as the older clutch is much stronger and more aggressive than the new arrivals. With a towel and clothespins I make a divider in the brooder, like a curtain, separating the two groups.

I had assumed there would be no practical way of maintaining dis-tinctions between the two family groups, but I am surprised to see that differences between the two clutches are discernible. The older group, clutch #2, is relatively dark; the yellow down is duller, the contrasting brown markings more conspicuous, and the heads much more elabo-rately streaked. By comparison, clutch #1 appears very yellow, the brown markings relatively pale, and the tops of their heads showing only a small amount of streaking. As time goes on, however, these dis-tinctions may become less obvious. There is an overlapping range of variation within each group, from lighter to darker, making the most pale individual in clutch #2 difficult to distinguish from the darkest of clutch #1.

May 14, Tuesday

I am awake before daylight and go straight to the incubator. The sick poult from the day before seems completely recovered, so I assume he ate something disagreeable. One more hatch from clutch #1 has just occurred, and as I set about interacting with this one, I see that the remaining two eggs are also on their way.

The two separate clutches in the brooder have moved together and are sleeping in one pile with the dividing towel bisecting the group. They become very vocal as I peer into the box. We are all glad to be reunited.

I suddenly see a poult stumbling in the brooder and recognize that one has become spraddle legged. As the newcomers slept in a tight pile, this one's legs must have been pressed in such a way, and for a sufficient period of time, to produce the condition. All were perfectly normal the night before. It is a pitiful sight.

Nervous about losing young wild turkeys, I have purchased a roll of half-inch-mesh poultry wire, twenty-four inches wide by fifty feet long. I doubled the wire over for rigidity, making it a stiff twelve inches wide. I can now place it anywhere, creating a comfortably large wire circle in which we can sit and forage. There is a weedy area behind my yard that looks to me like excellent wild turkey habitat, so I set up the wire circle and retrieve both clutches from the brooder, including little "spraddle legs," using a towel-lined cardboard box. As we begin exploring this interesting new environment within the circle, I soon realize that the wire is unnecessary and serves principally to contain my own anxiety.

Little spraddle legs can barely walk, and standing is impossible. When he sits the condition is made worse by his own weight forcing his legs and feet farther apart. I try holding him in my hand and with my fingers force his "knocked knees" (which, of course, are not knees but rather the joint of the tarsus and the tibia) apart and hold his feet crossed. After a few minutes I place him on the ground, and he walks more naturally. When he stops walking, however, his feet immediately go out, his knees come together, and he is forced to sit down in the spraddled position. I hold him once again, repeating the positioning of the legs and stretching them until I feel a slight tension on the tendons. This apparently causes no discomfort to the little turkey, and, eventually, he falls sound asleep in my hand.

I hold the little turkey for an hour or so, and I am heartened to see that when placed on the ground again, he walks in a normal manner. I try to reinforce this, nudging him along, strengthening the affected muscles by forcing him to walk. This seems to improve his condition still further. I continue with him in this way for the remainder of the day.

Although the weather during the day is very pleasant (probably in the low 80s), I notice that the poults are easily chilled, apparently dependent on either the hen or direct sunshine to maintain adequate body heat. When they enter a shady area they quickly begin to shiver and become lethargic, preferring to sit in the company of others or with me.

Even in the brooder they become chilled if they stray too far from the heating lamp, but there they know to immediately return to the light.

We return to the brooder after a few hours, to find that three of the young ones that I transferred from the incubator this morning have gotten wet from falling into the narrow rim of the waterer. Two are so chilled that they shake and stagger. The third is down and cannot open his eyes. I immediately place the three in the incubator. I am finding it nearly impossible to adequately care for so many turkeys in three different stages of development. Fortunately, by 11:30 A.M. the last of clutch #1 has hatched. There are no eggs left in clutch #1, and the remaining four eggs in clutch #2, I conclude, are definitely not going to produce.

I take the four remaining eggs outside and carefully open one. The heat of the incubator has dried the egg internally, and it looks like an egg that has been hard boiled. It is uniformly pale yellow inside with no apparent separation between the yolk and the albumen, smelling slightly musty but not objectionable. I find the others to be in a similar undifferentiated state and conclude that either they were sterile or development was arrested very early—long before they arrived at my door.

The three chilled poults in the incubator are fluffy and sleeping soundly together. The last of the hatchlings are likewise doing well, and I spend time interacting with them. I was fortunate to have attended every hatch.

Of the twenty-three eggs that have hatched, twenty-two are surviving in good condition. I break down the success rate of the hatch as follows:

Hatching Success

	Clutch #1	Clutch #2
Clutch size	16	13
Number eggs incubated	15	13
Began incubation	May 3, 1:00 A.M.	May 7, 6:00 P.M.
First hatch	May 13, 8:00 A.M.	May 10, 5:00 P.M.
Last hatch	May 14, 11:30 A.M.	May 11, 5:00 P.M.
Total hours hatching	27 ½	24

	Clutch #1	Clutch #2
Number of sterile eggs	1	4
Number of dead eggs	1	none
Mortality first 24 hours	none	1
Number of hatchlings	14	9
Total		23

The entire hatching process involved approximately ninety hours from the first hatch until the last, slightly less than four days. To me it feels like one very long day, and I realize that I have slept only a few hours. Imprinting seems to be well accomplished, and I look forward to a good night of sleep. A real meal would be nice—perhaps breakfast, a visit with Claudia.

May 15, Wednesday

The little spraddle-legged poult has completely recovered and cannot be distinguished from the rest. All of the turkeys appear very alert. The last of the hatch was placed in the brooder last night, and they have integrated nicely. The poults who became chilled yesterday are perfectly well today and seem in no way impaired by their ordeal. They join the rest in the brooder.

It is a rainy and dreary day, and although there are occasional breaks, I do not want to risk getting anyone chilled in the wet grass. The air is cool and damp, and the lack of sunshine would surely prove stressful to the little birds. It appears to me that, excepting predation, the combined effects of moisture and chill are probably the most dangerous obstacles to the survival of very young wild turkeys. It is amazing to me that wild turkey populations thrive in areas such as the Big Horn Mountains of Wyoming, where nights are never warm and snowfall may persist into June. It is testimony to the resilience of young wild turkeys and to the well-developed ability of the hen to protect her young. Williams points out, however, that, according to recent research, the limiting effects of cold and moisture on the survival of wild turkey poults may not be as severe as previously thought;

disease, facilitated by cold stress, may be more directly responsible for mortality.

We spend a large part of the day interacting in the brooder. The little turkeys appear perfectly content; they seem very comfortable and casually go about their small turkey business, which involves much preening, stretching, eating, chasing an occasional insect that is attracted to the light, and, of course, sleeping. These young turkeys sleep sprawled out like old hound dogs before a fire, acting as though their needs are perfectly met and projecting an air that I interpret as a joyful but reserved optimism.

I try to maintain as much direct eye contact and physical interaction as possible by keeping in close proximity to the brooder. As I sit on my cushion and overlook everyone, a poult will periodically approach and confront me directly by peering up into my eyes, which are only inches from his tiny face. He will intently stare, motionless, straight on, for what seems a very long time, without interruption, then carry on normal behavior. I am not certain, but it seems that each one eventually finds an opportunity for this, and that all, or most, have displayed this curious behavior. It is as though they are trying to absorb something. It appears to be a very conscious behavior and one that is testing a very small attention span. Perhaps it is a component of the imprinting process. Being the object of such intense scrutiny by such a little thing is a strange sensation.

I change the towels that line the bottom of the brooder regularly. Three towels are rotated, and as one becomes dirty (not unlike a diaper), it is replaced. I hose off the dirty towels and then wash them. They become sufficiently soiled to warrant changing about three times a day. The brooder needs to be as clean as possible. I intentionally chose older, faded towels in varying earth tones. Two are brown—one light, the other dark—and the third is a plaid of two natural shades of green. Knowing that birds in general are sensitive to color, I hoped that these towels would be regarded with indifference by the poults.

This afternoon I noticed that the towel in the brooder needed changing, but neither of the two replacements was dry. Thoughtlessly, I retrieved another towel and replaced the dirty one, using a systematic method I devised so as to disturb everyone as little as possible.

Immediately halting all activity, the poults pressed into one corner of the brooder with heads raised high. At first, I thought they were merely reacting to the disturbance of the change, but as this behavior persisted, I recognized it must be the color of the new towel, which was a rather obnoxious bright blue, a color that could only be ignored (or worse, appreciated) by an organism with a diminished or impaired sensory awareness. I ran back into the house and found a clean brown towel, and the poults' behavior returned to normal as soon as it was installed in the brooder.

The storms subside in the late afternoon, allowing the sun to shine for a few hours. The temperature is again comfortable, and so we take advantage of the opportunity to forage for a while within the wire circle. The turkeys seem to be very vigorous, stimulated by the warm dampness of the land, and they are becoming much more aggressive in pursuit of small insects, which are abundant after the rains.

When I return the poults to their brooder, they immediately gather together and fall asleep. I remain with them until well after dark, eventually sneaking quietly into the house.

May 16, Thursday

A single, contiguous mass of wild turkey down divides and separates into its individual components, each of which is defined by a pair of piercing black eyes. A small cheer goes up from the crowd when I appear a few minutes before sunrise. Everyone appears healthy and enthusiastic. Immediately, feeding and exploring activities are resumed within the brooder, accompanied by much stretching and flapping of tiny wings, which, remarkably, have grown noticeably longer in the night. Tiny tail feathers are similarly making their appearance through the thick down of the little birds. Likewise, I notice that the poults are losing their sleepy newborn appearance, rapidly replacing it with an alertness in their eyes and a general air of awareness.

It is a damp, pleasantly cool morning, which is very refreshing to me but might not be good for the turkeys, so I will wait until the sun is well up before going out to the wire circle. I enjoy a hot cup of coffee while hanging over the brooder, talking, and exchanging occasional intense stares. I find myself grinning uncontrollably as these little turkeys display a gravity that is completely disproportional to their size and age. They have grown noticeably in these few days. The older ones measure about four and a half inches tall in a normal standing posture.

The turkeys definitely are becoming more aggressive by the minute. As I sit in the wire circle, I am surrounded by a small but vigorous industry. Being a small wild turkey is a serious business; they invest themselves totally in their occupation, and every moment seems to be payday. Theirs is an ongoing and constantly varying agenda of responsibilities. There is dusting to be done, and an abandoned anthill serves the job perfectly. Dusting is done prostrate, generally on one side, and involves much kicking and flapping about to systematically draw sand and dust up into the feathers. They seem to take great pleasure in it. Each one, or groups of two or three, takes a turn on the hill and dusts off and on until the hill is leveled and the dirt left pocked with tiny, bowl-shaped impressions the size of small wild turkey bodies. Sunlight must also be gathered, and they are hungry for it. It is difficult for them to pass a warm patch of this stuff without some effort to absorb it by stretching out on the ground. Judging by the amount of time if not effort, spent in this pursuit, I now know wild turkeys to be composed of a large proportion of sunshine. Protein is also of great importance in their development, and its acquisition seems to be the primary focus of activity. Today I try to observe closely and identify the objects of so much attention.

Wild turkeys are hunters and predators in their own right, and although some of these poults are still timid, I see them carefully stalking and often catching a variety of insects: various flies, gnats, ants, leaf hoppers, small black field crickets, and small grasshoppers. Considerable time is spent in shaking the latter two, making certain that they are completely dead before swallowing them. Large crickets and grasshoppers are regarded with caution, and I actually saw and heard a poult's small but perfectly enunciated staccato alarm putt as he marked the location of a particularly large grasshopper. It is interesting also to note that certain insects of seemingly perfect dimensions for eating are totally and without question disregarded as potential meals. The common black spittle bug with three transverse, narrow pink bands is one of those. Another that is ignored or "tasted" and rejected is the common love bug. Having inadvertently eaten a few love bugs myself, I can attest to their lack of palatability. Bees and wasps appear to be invisible or are barely acknowledged. Small slugs and earthworms have come to the surface of the damp ground. The slugs are readily taken by the turkeys, but the larger earthworms are regarded with interest and caution. The smallest worms are eaten by some turkeys after an extremely long period of time spent trying to kill them by shaking them against the ground. Small spiders are eaten enthusiastically, but larger ones, like the wolf spiders, are either considered frightening or ignored. Millipedes are pecked at but not eaten. Small centipedes are shaken vigorously and eaten. A large variety of seeds—those that have fallen to the ground and those that still reside on plants—are eagerly eaten. I also see them beginning to eat sand and grit, which are necessary for digestion.

An hour or two of this frenetic activity and they are left temporarily exhausted. Sleeping is another business, at which they are very accomplished. As I sit cross-legged on the ground, they all press in around me and become quiet. I find at these times that my eyes become heavy, and there is a contagion in their slumber that produces a corresponding languor in me. At one point I was forced to lie with my head on the ground, surrounded by a warm pillow of downy wild turkeys. I have no idea how long we dozed, and I was awakened only upon being pecked on the lip by a little one who had been sleeping on my chest.

One of the poults has somehow injured his tail and is attracting attention. The others are attempting to remove the injury by pecking at it constantly, making things even worse. A couple of the poults actually have blood on their bills.

Regretfully, I isolate the injured poult from the group, using another small towel-lined cardboard box supplied with food and water. I clean the injury with hydrogen peroxide and place the poult in the box. He immediately begins "lost calling," making a loud and desperate *peep peep peep* meant to call the hen from long distances. Fortunately, he is only inches from the others, and their vocalizations serve as some consolation. He eats and drinks and appears to be strong. I will have to keep him isolated until his injuries are completely healed.

This little turkey also has a middle toe on his left foot that curves inward, but this anomaly in no way impedes his ability to walk. There are two other turkeys with an outside toe that curves inward and under the foot in such a way that they are forced to stand on the bent toes. As I did with the spraddle-legged poult, I spend time holding these individuals and forcing the bent toes into the correct placement, which seems to improve the condition, if only temporarily. The bones in the feet are very soft and flexible. Perhaps these deformities will eventually correct themselves as the feet grow stronger. In any case, the little turkeys seem to enjoy being held in this way and sleep contentedly in my hand.

May 17, Friday

After deliberating for several days, I have decided that the plantation is an inappropriate place to raise a flock of wild turkeys. There is a constant whir of human activity here with maintenance activities on the grounds, as well as a continuous parade of cars, trucks, and tractors. I would like to insulate the turkeys from as much human activity as possible. Likewise, the presence of many dogs, both in pens and free roaming, makes our activities here impossible. Therefore, I have chosen to move the turkeys tonight to a location that will afford us solitude and relative safety, as well as access to almost unlimited wild lands on which we can roam and grow.

Claudia and I own a small piece of property bordering the Apalachicola National Forest, sixteen acres of undeveloped land that is part of an old abandoned farm. Here we share weekends and long summer breaks away from her teaching routine in the local county— Wakulla. She has named the property Wren Nest. There is a small but comfortable, well-equipped cabin there and no other "improvements" on the land. It is a quarter-mile drive to a national forest graded road and another half mile to one of the only paved roads in the area.

At almost seven days old, the little turkeys are already beginning to experiment with flight, and this will surely be accomplished in only a day or two. They are rapidly outgrowing the makeshift brooder, and so we cannot wait. As the turkeys sleep in a single pile, I notice that the size of their mass has grown considerably relative to the area of the brooder.

In the cover of darkness we will leave for Wren Nest tonight in hopes that, without light, the move will not be too disturbing to the turkeys. Yesterday I purchased the materials for a pen, by phone, and had them delivered. I will begin construction tomorrow.

PART II

The house at Wren Nest is built on low pilings in the mesic hardwood hammock that borders a beautiful limestone-bottom stream draining out of the national forest and the southern end of Bradwell Bay National Wilderness Area. The stream is called Mill Creek in reference to a gristmill that was situated on it and served a community named Greenough in the mid- to late 1800s. With the exception of some debris at the mill site, there is not so much as a brick to indicate that the community ever existed.

Years ago, I was shown the location of an unmarked cemetery by the old sage and farmer who struggled with this land for the best part of a hundred years. It was he, Bert Rhoddenbery, who sold me property here over twenty years ago. He was part genius and part lighter knot—hard and combustible—and I have never known a man possessed of more genuine wisdom. The first time I met Mr. Bert, he surprised me in the woods as I was exploring Mill Creek and asked me if I had seen a spotted hog. I had not seen his hog, but I did find a friend.

Today the cemetery site is marked by a large hickory tree and the only patch of palmettos Mr. Bert would allow to survive on "good high ground," saying this was the site of the old Greenough log church. Mr. Bert somehow lived well on a land that would have impoverished the average cotton rat, but then he and his wife, Cora, were willing in their eighties to put on their baseball caps backward and hoe thirty acres of corn by hand. He had an old Farmall tractor, one of those clanking, indestructible products of the post–industrial revolution, which worked perfectly, but he preferred to plow with his mule because he said she ran better. Bert and Cora passed on many years ago, but when I walk these woods and grown-over fields, I see signs of him every-where: an old stretch of broken-down fence, a chop mark where he tested the integrity of an ancient heart-pine post, or a rusty fence staple slowly disappearing into the bark of an aged live oak.

Mr. Bert, through his ingenuity, managed to extract from the land anything and everything of any value. But, I intended to reap a differ-ent sort of harvest, one that would yield an intangible wealth—a bounty of sight and sound, of discovery and experience. With its unlimited red maple and gallberry, thousands upon thousands of fragrant wild aza-leas, this land is an environmental exchange where a bull would starve but a bear might flourish, where nothing moves fast but the many rapids and waterfalls in the limestone-bottom creeks. It is the only place I have ever known where coral snakes may be said to be abundant, where the underside of every sweet bay leaf is lined with silver, where security surrounds the large diamonds that adorn the backs of many solitary rattlesnakes, and where in autumn golden asters bloom in such profusion that they could not be counted in a lifetime. These old swamps, hammocks, and exhausted flatwoods constituted for me, at $250 an acre, the bargain of a lifetime.

Immediately upon arriving at Wren Nest, I must set to work building a pen for the turkeys. Until the poults are old enough to be relatively safe from predators, they will need a refuge in which to stay at night and at times when I cannot be with them. Data regarding mortality in young wild turkeys is information that I do not need. I already know that they can die in large numbers.

The pen I build must serve to house the turkeys comfortably and have enough room to permit limited flight. And it must exclude predators from above, on the ground, and even below the ground.

The pen will be sixteen feet wide by twenty-four feet long by eight feet high. The framework will consist of pressure-treated 4x4 posts set on eight-foot centers, buried four feet in the ground and extending eight feet above. The width of the pen will be spanned overhead with sixteen-foot-long 2x8s placed at four-foot intervals, and those joists will be joined between by perpendicular 2x4s set on edge running the length of the pen at four-foot intervals. These will provide anchorage for the one-inch-mesh poultry wire that will cover the entire pen, top and bottom, and extend a foot into the ground all the way around. This will exclude raccoons, coyotes, dogs, and even bears that could try to dig under the fence. I'll reinforce the lower portion of the pen with 2x4 inch mesh welded wire fencing that will extend from one foot below ground to three feet above ground and attach to a 2x4 perline placed two feet above the ground between the posts and running entirely around the pen. The gate to the pen will be a substantial hinged 2x4-and-wire door, framed and fitted tightly. One corner of the pen will have a simple, sloping roof, eight feet by eight feet, which will provide a dry area during wet times. The roof, of course, is not something that turkeys would enjoy in the wild, but until they obtain more mature plumage, it may be of some importance. I, unlike the turkey hen, cannot afford them any protection when roosting. Feeders, waterers, and tree limbs around the corners of the pen for roosting will be the final touches.

May 18, Saturday

Normally, thrashing around with a pile of framing lumber is something that I would enjoy doing on a Saturday morning. I suppose I am one of those peculiar people who thrives on manual labor. I would rather split wood than eat. Any other time, I would face this stack of lumber and wire with pleasure, but today I should be spending time with the young birds. This is the most formative period of their lives, and I feel that every minute is especially important to them. All I can do is try to divide my time between them and this construction. The pen must be completed as soon as possible.

The turkeys have already outgrown the makeshift plywood brooder and upon arrival were transferred to a commercial poultry brooder, which is roomy, warm, and clean. This will have to suffice while pen building is underway. I will alternately spend time with the turkeys in the wire circle or sitting on the edge of the field throughout the day.

I begin construction by running strings and putting down the 4x4 posts. By afternoon I am ready to hang the overhead joists. Snorrii Solburg, a neighbor and good friend, comes over in the afternoon to help me with this section of the pen, which goes up fast and very square. Claudia helps by sitting fifty yards away in the wire circle with the little poults while we drive nails. The poults seem to weather this noise and confusion very well. Claudia complains that the turkeys periodically "lost call," as they apparently differentiate her from me, but they are composed enough in her company to take water and rest. If, however, she should leave the wire circle, they become very upset, lost calling and constantly running back and forth against the fence. They never lost call if I am near.

The pen is being constructed just out of view of the cabin on the edge of the hammock that runs between Mill Creek and the margin of an old field that begins abruptly. The hardwoods of the mesic hammock nearby consist of live oak, water oak, laurel oak, sweet gum, pig nut hickory, magnolia, American holly, dogwood, and red bay. This zone, nearing the field, immediately gives way to loblolly pine, deer berry and other vacciniums, stagger bush, various seed-bearing grasses, blackberry, winged sumac, and a variety of smaller herbaceous plants that receive protection and moisture from the hammock. This narrow transition zone creates an integrated and diverse habitat that constitutes a richer and more complicated ecological community than either the hammock or the field.

As construction proceeds on the pen, I make a concerted effort to leave the area that will become the floor of the pen as undisturbed as possible, in order to allow the turkeys to take advantage of this relative abundance of plant and insect life. At least for a few days it should allow them an interesting and fruitful area in which to forage, and enough cover to make them feel secure.

Building a pen from scratch is essential, as an existing pen could expose the poults to ground previously contaminated by domestic birds. Wild turkeys are especially vulnerable to diseases carried by domestic poultry, and apparently the soil can retain pathogens dangerous to wild turkeys for a long time. Whole populations of wild turkeys have been decimated in the past by black head disease, for example, which can be transmitted by domestic turkeys.

This ground has probably never had domestic birds living on it and should be very clean. Our biggest worry should be from the resident wild turkey population and infection from their naturally occurring diseases. We should expect to encounter fowl pox, which reportedly is endemic to all wild turkey populations and must simply run its course in every young turkey.

After completing the framing, I proceed the following day with stretching the wire. Having a square framework makes this job relatively easy. I must, however, dig a ditch around the entire pen. The trench must be at least a foot deep and as wide as a shovel. This process is complicated by two large loblolly pines standing on either side and by numerous hardwoods on the back side, where the pen nestles into the hammock. The ground is full of roots, some quite large, and I spend considerable time with the ax.

As I continue working on the trench into the morning , I am obsessively compelled to make the edges straight. Cutting the profiles clean and vertical using my flat shovel, I admire the dark humus with flecks of charcoal as it fades gradually down to the more organically sterile yellow sand below. The dark stain of an ancient mole burrow winds serpentine across the bottom of the trench in the cool, moist soil. The rich, musty smell of the newly opened earth and the sharp perfume of fresh-cut pine roots envelop me in a past spent digging archaeological sites around Florida. Instinctively, as my shovel glides along the bottom of the trench, I feel for the telltale clink of flint, bone, or sherd. For a short time I am lost in this rectangular hole in the ground and lose sight of my objective. The ground and the past speak to me.

I nail a four-foot-wide strip of stiff, welded wire fence around the bottom of the pen and down into the trench, then begin back-filling and throwing dirt into the yawning ditch.

May 23, Thursday

After completing the door and placing sparkleberry limbs in the corners, I finally release the little turkeys from their brooder into the pen. Immediately, they set about exploring their new area. They are about a week and a half old and now fly very well. They are attracted to the limbs overhead, and each in turn flies up to see their world from this new vantage. Contrary to popular belief, these young wild turkeys seem in no way confused by the poultry wire surrounding the pen and recognize it as the limit of their explorations. Occasionally, one will make an airborne tour around the perimeter of the pen without ever colliding with the wire. Likewise, they seem uninclined to exit through the fence while on the ground.

I have released the little poult who was pecked, as well as one who appeared weak, and both have by now recovered nicely. The former is now wary of handling but still wants to remain close to me.

As the group slowly becomes accustomed once again to life outside the brooder and their curiosity regarding this new location is satisfied, their interest begins to focus more in my direction. Within an hour their exuberance wanes, and soon we are all sitting in a sleepy pile in dappled sunlight filtering through the large pines overhead. At last, all we have to do is set about the business of being wild turkeys. They obviously feel safe and comfortable, and at least for now the area of the pen affords them a whole world of opportunity.

Within the pen I have placed a waterer and poultry feeder filled with "starter." As of yesterday, I began to feed out two hundred live crickets a day, purchased at an area bait shop.

Periodically released on the ground, about fifty at a time, they are eagerly eaten. Live protein could be critical to young wild turkeys, and I want to compensate for any loss they may have suffered in the brooder.

The poults are remarkably alert. They are only a little over a week old, and yet they seem to exhibit a confidence and an awareness that at once includes the smallest crawling particle on a leaf and the red-tailed hawk soaring a half mile up the field. They acknowledge, in some way, any sound or occurrence in the area, so that a whir of interesting activity and behavior is unfolding around me constantly. I can see that it will be difficult for me to keep up.

It is broad daylight in midafternoon. A possum comes snooping up to the pen. Irresistibly attracted by either sight, sound, or smell, he sees only an easy meal and fails to notice me. I am suddenly outraged by even the thought of his intent and jump up and grab the nearest blunt object, which is a short piece of 4x4 lying just outside the pen. I chase him fifty yards across the lower corner of the field and finally toss the 4x4, which misses its mark but nevertheless impresses the plodding marsupial. I look back and see that the poults are standing together, each very tall and silent. I feel a little silly over the ferociousness of my reaction but am somewhat compensated by the notion that the possum will probably not be so cavalier in the future.

After we settle back down, I notice that each of the turkeys will on occasion stop and quietly gaze into the distance. Only eight days old and already developing the thousand-yard stare. I experiment with the alarm purr, which sends everyone diving for cover. From now on I will be much more careful to voice this call only when we or I encounter something perceived to be dangerous. Cautiously they emerge from their hiding and run to my side, and in a few moments their activity returns to normal.

May 24, Friday

The dawn is pleasant and a bit breezy, although rain is predicted for the afternoon. Summer is undoubtedly on its way. Yellow flies are

beginning to be a bother. The turkeys, however, treat them as tasty morsels and occasionally pluck one out of midair.

Although one corner of the pen is roofed with two pieces of treated plywood, I've decided to keep the poults in the brooder at night. Rainy nights in particular can still be cool, and until they are stronger, I will take no chances. Juvenile plumage is rapidly replacing their natal down and will serve to make them less vulnerable to dampness and chill.

Rather than taking the poults directly to the pen this morning, I find a spot on the edge of the old field, which is rougher than the environment of the pen and may provide better foraging. Also, the more time we spend out of the pen, the better preserved the environment within will remain.

The little poults seem delighted and energetic and immediately begin with small wild turkey activities. They are somewhat cautious and seem to recognize this as being an unknown area, but soon they are browsing and occasionally venturing several yards away. These small expeditions are short lived, however, and end with a nervous dash back to my side.

Not wanting to interfere with the turkeys' activities or their interaction with the natural world, I attempt to be inconspicuous and hide, sitting under some low pine boughs and thick deer berry. As the sun reaches the tops of the trees across the field on the eastern horizon, I watch comfortably as the small wild turkeys preen, dust, sleep, and explore the interesting tufts of grass on the field's edge. It is a beautiful scene, and I cannot help but feel a little smug about how this experiment is going.

The field and surrounding hammock are pulsing with the hypnotic drone of insects. The repetitive overlapping voices of several species of warbler combine to gently weave a warm blanket of experience. The words of Joseph Campbell quietly overtake me: "Illumination is the recognition of the radiance of one eternity through all things." Even the mosquito that softly hums past my ear seems amiable and a part of this rhythmic resonating dance of sight and sound. The air is heavy and moist. Dew hangs in sparkling droplets in rows along the sagging webs of spiders. Their nocturnal business complete, the spiders too sit in idle repose under overhanging leaves. I feel a comfortable lull of my cognitive faculties. My eyelids sag like the morning spider's silk.

An abrupt chatter and simultaneous explosive blur of wings! My body recoils involuntarily. I blink and the dark shape mantling only a few feet before me rotates, exposing two large piercing eyes. Instantly, the great hawk springs into the air and, as he lifts, I see a lump drop immediately to the ground. As if pulled by the backwash of powerful wings, I find myself on all fours staring down on the lifeless body of a small wild turkey, warm and limp in my hand.

Sickened, I begin calling to the others, who have scattered all around. Momentarily, I hear faint lost calling in the hammock behind me. I yelp softly, and a poult bolts from his hiding place a few feet away and runs under my legs. Others begin running back, and soon all seem to be reassembled. Some peer cautiously with long, craning necks at the spiritless form lying in the grass nearby. I gather everyone up, and we walk directly back to the pen.

As I sit on the grassy floor of the pen and fumble with these field notes, the little turkeys stay close and are subdued; they preen and sleep. I am disgusted and embarrassed over what has occurred. I could have anticipated this. The last thing I should do is try to conceal myself while in the field with week-old wild turkeys. Until these birds are bigger and stronger, we will stay in the pen. Such predation is not something that I wanted to include in this experience.

So as not to accustom the local predators to the taste of young wild turkey, I go bury the unlucky little thing, who has paid the price for my thoughtlessness. I can still see those fierce, amber eyes. The hawk was magnificent. Like a humiliating chess move that I failed to anticipate, he has come from nowhere and taken my queen.

May 26, Sunday

The weather has turned disagreeable, and we have rain day and night. The ground is saturated, and I am concerned about the environment in the pen becoming unhealthy. In addition to it being a breeding ground for disease, the young poults are still rather downy and so manage to get wet while foraging. On occasion they seem to get chilled, and I frequently opt to load them back into the brooder, even though I consider every minute spent there as time wasted and opportunities missed for the turkeys' growth and development. The moisture and humidity have likewise caused the insects to emerge in great numbers. Deer flies,

yellow flies, mosquitoes, and gnats are all thriving. The word in the flatwoods has always been that a wet spring means a poor wild turkey crop for the year. It is a dreary time, and we all stay wet most of the day.

This soil is sandy and porous. Rainwater passes through it unimpeded, like a solvent, to the shallow karst bedrock below. It then sheets across the rock and reappears in the form of springheads along the slopes of the various creeks and drainages. The cycle from total saturation to drought is completed in only a few days, and two weeks without significant rainfall leaves the land and its vegetation parched. This is a land that loves to be wet. It would rather be a swamp, but it must console itself with only intermittent and occasional inundation. The hammocks and flatwoods rejoice and prosper in this condition until even the air begins to look green. By day, this is the time of the algae and the fungus, the liverwort, the lichen, and the moss. By night, nine different species of frogs and toads unite in a deafening primeval anthem. Combined with the drone of nocturnal insects, it is an atavistic celebration and a resurgent liberation of snails, slugs, and all others lacking a highly centralized nervous system—an exultation of invertebrates, to which I am only potential anchorage, damp but high ground, and source for a possible meal. The land slowly exhales its warm verdant breath—the vapor of pungent organic decomposition and sweet vegetative growth. Rain and sweat both periodically splatter my field notes—ink and thoughts run wild and blurry. A tick meanders across my hand, weaving through small droplets of water. A mosquito hangs upside down from the visor of my cap—we share a small dark refuge and our point of view is identical.

I am discovering daily how sensitive young wild turkeys are to color. It appears that in particular the violet end of the spectrum is significant to them, and many of those colors can be distracting or disturbing. The turkeys are very concerned about my appearance and my choice of clothing. Colors of red or purple are totally unacceptable; strangely, they also find a particular beige shirt annoying and will try to remove it.

My faded blue jeans, however, seem to go unnoticed except for the copper rivets and buttons, which continue to be a curiosity. Likewise, I have a number of faded blue T-shirts, which seem not to attract their attention. I cannot help but speculate that these pale blue colors approximate the coloring on the head of a wild turkey hen and therefore do not represent anything curious or disturbing. Additionally, I notice that if I wear shoes or boots with which they are unfamiliar, those also prove to be a source of distraction. Shoelaces, regardless, are distracting, and the turkeys are never completely accepting of them. My faded blue jeans and blue T-shirts will hereafter be my uniform, in an effort to allow the young turkeys to ignore me and concentrate as much as possible on the complicated business of being wild turkeys.

May 29, Wednesday

While putting some finishing touches on the outside of the pen, I see that if I am not sitting directly with the poults, they are frantic. They will lost call and run up and down the fence until I reenter the pen and join them. Likewise, they refuse to eat, drink water, or rest. In fact, I have noticed on at least one occasion that after a short time without me, they will run until they are completely exhausted.

Perhaps when these birds become stronger, they can spend time alone, but it is clear that for now I must be with them at all times. The exception to this is when they are in the brooder at night. Apparently, the warm confines of the brooder allow the turkeys to feel secure enough to eat and rest. In any case, for some unforeseen time to come I will be right here, and it is no longer an issue in my mind.

May 30, Thursday

I was shocked yesterday to be alerted by the turkeys to the presence of a large and ambitious gray rat snake. The six-foot snake passed through the one-inch mesh of the fence as though it were not there.

Although they were cautious, with craning necks and alarm putts, I thought the poults' reaction lacked the level of wariness I would like to see. I tried to reinforce the gravity of the situation with an alarm purr, which sent everyone dashing to my side. I then got up and caught the snake, which was obviously confusing for them but caused no panic. I placed the snake in a bag for safekeeping until I could carry him far away.

This morning another large gray rat snake casually slid through the fence. He joined the other in the sack. An hour later I am astonished to hear alarm putts and see another rat snake several feet outside the pen and headed our way. This is incredible. I see an occasional gray rat snake in these woods, but I had no idea there could be so many large ones in one area. And what could be so attractive to them? Perhaps it could be the particular movement of so many small birds. A possibility might also be scent, but I think that is less likely. Gray rat snakes are keen observers of the comings and goings of birds. They are frequently attracted to the periodic activity around bird nests, and on more than one occasion I have observed one coiled around a hummingbird feeder waiting for the next small arrival.

I am reminded of a distant summer spent in rearing a small family of human-imprinted wood ducks. Although made considerably more complicated than the current project by the logistical problem of living in the water, it was also fraught with reptile encounters. Spending day after day often submerged up to my nose in water afforded insight into the fascinating life of the wood duck and the interesting adversarial relationship that that species shares with the alligator. A summer of cat and mouse in water as black as coffee caused me to gain enormous respect for the alligator's prowess as a predator. I observed one particular alligator day after day as he systematically attempted to dine on baby duck. I was amazed to see that he employed various strategies that often involved great patience and restraint and also apparently some degree of abstract reasoning of the type one would associate with mammalian predators. On several occasions the alligator actually got to within three or four feet of me. I would suddenly realize that he was next to me in the water and would have no idea how long he had been there. If alligators were more inclined toward people than young ducks, we would be absolutely defenseless.

Fortunately, wood ducks seem to have a specific genetic programming for dealing with the alligator. If a young wood duck can survive his first encounter with an alligator, he appears to become relatively alligator-proof thereafter. As time went on, I learned to rely solely on wood duck perception for locating alligators.

Snakes and reptiles in general, while appearing dull witted, are undoubtedly much more aware than we like to give them credit for. People are probably consoled by the notion of the unintelligent snake and loath to imagine the one that could be clever. I have always thought that snakes are wonderful and have never been able to keep my hands off them. But for now, I wish they would just leave us alone.

June 1, Saturday

It is the weekend, and Claudia is here. As I sit with the birds, enjoying a relatively cool summer's morning, I notice them all standing tall, silent, and motionless. I look toward the cabin and eventually see Claudia walking toward us. She arrives and casually announces: "I think there's a bear in the yard." I jump up and walk cautiously from the pen thinking black hog, Labrador retriever, et cetera. But it is a bear all right, and upon seeing me, he dives into an impenetrable gallberry thicket east of the cabin. Wanting to get a look when he exits from the other side, I sprint around and follow a path down toward Mill Creek. Panting, I wait and listen—but no bear. I quietly walk to the creek and follow it up until I meet Claudia coming down from the other direction. She has not seen or heard anything, either. I suggest she wait there while I go back and take another path that dead-ends in the gallberry thicket. I sneak up the path, and there he is. He crashes through the thicket and trots within twenty feet of Claudia. She is impressed with his big ears. I am impressed with a track left in some mud excavated by a burrowing crayfish. The turkeys are just impressed.

We are fortunate in this part of Florida to have a population of black bears. Although I have seen their tracks on occasion for years and at one point even maintained a bear feeder (an inherently bad idea), this is the first time I have actually seen one on this property. I imagine him to be a young male pioneering new territory.

The margin between the hammock and the field is a corridor for wildlife moving about the area. Sitting within the confines of the pen all day allows us to survey all the traffic that can occur in one small region. In addition to those predatory individuals that are being drawn by the young turkeys, there is a parade of others just passing by. We average one or two box turtles a day, which the poults regard with suspicion. Yesterday a small chicken turtle wandered by quite far from the nearest pond. Black racers glide past several times a day, obviously on hunting expeditions, but are in no way attracted to or interested in young wild turkeys. Interestingly, even though on occasion the racers inadvertently pass through the pen, the turkeys, although cautious, seem to recognize them as being less threatening than the rat snakes.

A shy and beautiful coral snake passes through one corner of the pen. He is nosing through the leaf mulch and appears oblivious to the stir he has created among the young birds. Exercising great restraint, I refrain from handling this living jewelry. I am afraid of setting a bad example and so keep my hands to myself. We watch as he alternately appears and disappears in the dried magnolia leaves behind the pen. Eventually, the gentle little snake vanishes in the warm moist blanket of leaves on the hammock floor.

All manner of birds pass by at various times during the day. Some, like the cardinals and jays, exhibit great curiosity about the young turkeys. Likewise, the turkeys seem to show keen interest in all of the avian activity around them. Anything soaring overhead, regardless of how imperceptibly high, brings about immediate cautionary behaviors. Many times it is only with great difficulty that I locate some telescopic speck silently moving across the sky.

We also encounter a parade of insects, which frequently have the misfortune of blindly stumbling into the pen. Crickets, grasshoppers, spiders, and most anything with wings are unceremoniously seized and eaten. The poults can still be very cautious, however, when handling large spiders or grasshoppers. Many species are still deliberately ignored. Millipedes, which appear benign, are completely ignored, whereas centipedes, which reportedly are capable of a painful bite, are relished. The larger wolf spiders are now being eaten, but I notice that the poults handle them with great care until they are completely dead, and only then are they swallowed.

At about three weeks, these young wild turkeys are growing like weeds in plowed ground. Juvenile flight feathers seem to be fully emerged, with secondary coverts rapidly covering the upper wing. Likewise, the tertial series is well developed. Flight now is strong and deliberate, with excellent control over departures and landings. Small wild turkeys are now landing and standing around on my shoulders and head much of the time.

When relating directly to me, the poults prefer it eye to eye. While they are sleeping, they have a need to be actually touching me in some way. Presumably, they are secure in knowing that should I move or become startled, they would be immediately alerted.

Significant size differences exist now within the group. They range from six to eight inches in height. I have for a time worried that some

are developing poorly, although now I am beginning to suspect that I am already seeing some sexual dimorphism. Several of the poults from the dark clutch are particularly small. I also notice some faint bald spots on the heads of a few of the larger individuals—possibly males.

Overall their juvenile plumage is closing in, particularly across the back. The turkeys now spend a large portion of their time attending to this emerging plumage, which involves as much dusting and preening as weather permits.

Certain innate social behaviors are also well emerged. Strutting is common, along with a host of other behaviors such as aggressive postures, intense eye contact, lying prostate with neck outstretched, or moving briskly away, which are used to express dominance, submission, and avoidance. Roles are entirely interchangeable, it seems, and submission accompanied by mock mounting behavior occurs on occasion. Fighting, although fairly common now, lacks any grave intent.

I continue to feed them two hundred crickets per day and also provide fresh greens, including sorrel, kale, romaine, spinach, and tender smilax tips that I gather in the nearby hammock. Turkey starter feed is being eaten in ever-increasing amounts. Although the poults appear to be developing very well, the fear of disease constantly looms in the back of my mind. I worry when I observe any turkey being particularly sleepy or lethargic. They still are at a tender age, and it is obvious that they can be easily stressed by overexertion in the heat or by dampness and cold.

An interesting cohesion between the group and myself has developed. There is a trust and predictability, an ease and comfort in our interaction. In spite of this unusual kinship of wild birds and man, we are experiencing something that feels, curiously, normal.

June 2, Sunday

The first week of June, in the North Florida flatwoods, is by any definition a hard time. Rains have fallen intermittently for days. In spite of the cloud cover and humidity the temperature remains high, and when the sun appears, the temperature moves immediately into the high 90s. Evaporation is now only theoretical, and so the human cooling system is inefficient. Though the young wild turkeys are also stressed under these uncomfortable circumstances, they seem to tolerate the conditions better than I.

Local flatwoods wisdom has it that the yellow fly appears as blackberries first set their fruit and then persists until the ripe fruit disappears. Blooms have dropped, and we can see the hard red fruit dotted here and there through the heavy summer air. Yellow flies are in full bloom and arrive in periodic silent menacing squadrons, flashing wary iridescent green eyes. They are in fact rather handsome insects, but familiarity quickly breeds contempt. They appear in fast-moving groups of six or eight individuals, and soon you find that you are forced to surrender all of your attention to them, for to ignore the silent horde is to ensure a painful and lingering bite to the finger, the elbow, or—the worst—the lip. They manage even to find an occasional meal on the legs of the poults. I kill hundreds, and the poults help me quickly dispose of the dead. The flies seem to prosper and become particularly vicious when the heat and humidity are high and the air is still and overcast. Mosquitoes and gnats are also numerous but pale to insignificance when the yellow fly flourishes.

I have just learned that some domestic poultry in various areas of Wakulla County has recently been tested and found to be carrying equine encephalitis. This disease can be transmitted by insects to humans with potentially fatal results. I am transfused many times each day as various species of bloodsucking insects find their repast interrupted by an alert poult and so then choose to complete their meal on my ear. I reluctantly share my blood with these birds, imagining all sorts of amusing epitaphs to explain the somewhat unusual, if not ridiculous, nature of my departure, should it occur.

It is midday on Sunday, and Claudia's parents have come to Wren Nest for lunch and an afternoon visit. Wishing to be sociable and have a bug-free meal, I choose to make a quick trip into the cabin for a sandwich and something with ice in it. I glance quickly around the ground surrounding the pen and dash to the house, trying to ignore the pleading lost calls behind me.

I hurriedly eat my sandwich, and suddenly thunder crashes nearby. Running to the pen, hoping to return the poults to their brooder before the storm, I see everyone crowded into the far corner of the pen. As I enter the door of the pen, my eye is drawn to a gray linear shape to my left. I stand in disbelief as I realize that a large gray rat snake has completely eaten a young turkey and is now trapped within the pen. The enormous lump in his midsection will not permit his exit through the fence.

Bewildered and addled, I put the indifferent snake and his precious cargo into the sack with another snake caught the day before. I gather the survivors and return them to their brooder as rain clatters through the magnolia leaves in the hammock.

The poults are nearly one month old. I thought they were too strong and much too large to be eaten by a snake, although I have feared that they could still be captured and killed by one. I have underestimated the lethal potential of the snake. It seems as though some clever conspiracy has occurred and that this snake could only have been patiently waiting for a window of opportunity to make his sinister move.

Until they are much too large for snakes, I will never leave them alone again. And since they are outgrowing the brooder, I'll need to construct a snake-proof enclosure within the pen for protection at night until they are old enough to roost outside.

June 7, Friday

With half-inch-mesh hardware cloth and pressure-treated 2x2 lumber, I construct a roomy snake-proof enclosure, five feet long, three feet wide, and two feet high. It is simply a wire box with a top that is completely removable and held down by gravity. It will rest on the ground, under the dry roof. I will be relieved to have the poults out of the brooder and not have to worry about snakes. And it should be simple to rig for warmth. It is the night of June 7, and the weather has suddenly turned unseasonably cool with a stiff breeze from the northeast. With a light for heat and a blanket over the snake-proof cage, the poults should be comfortable during their first night in the pen.

I remain with them well into the evening until I am certain that the new enclosure is not disorienting or frightening for them. They appear content and after some obligatory exploration soon come to rest in a nodding pile under the warm light and as close to me as they can get. Eventually, after dark, I sneak quietly into the cabin, longing for the day when we can head out and leave all of this behind.

In the evenings, I usually spend some time organizing my field notes. Occasionally I will go into town to run errands, and nights are my only opportunity for a substantial meal. Due to the poults' extreme curiosity about my behavior, I find it impossible to eat anything while in their presence.

June 9, Sunday

The weather has at last improved. The humidity is down around 70 percent, the temperature is in the high 80s, and the air is stirring. Alert, bright eyed, and strong, these young wild turkeys seem to be in great shape. They are growing fast, and change occurs daily. They are slightly over one month old now, and their juvenile plumage appears to be complete. Juvenile plumage in young wild turkeys has been described as resembling that of a female pheasant. That seems to be an accurate description of coloration, markings, and in the case of the larger individuals, who now stand one foot tall, size.

I am beginning to see evidence of the third molt, technically referred to as the first-basic or post-juvenile molt by Williams and Austin. Third-molt feathers in wild turkeys superficially resemble those of the adult. This molt, plus the partial molt known as prealternate, must see the maturing bird through to the following spring, when the true adult plumage will begin to emerge. The adult will receive a new, complete addition of feathers each year thereafter, throughout his life. Feathers are shed and replaced in predictable processions, and every wild turkey molts in the same order as every other. Lovett Williams has explored this somewhat complicated process in great detail. Aldo Starker Leopold also conducted a study of feather development in wild and domestic turkeys in 1943.

Rich brown tail coverts have been the first visible sign of the third molt. I am now beginning to see juvenile tail feathers and secondary flight feathers dropped here and there about the pen. The lower legs, or tarsi, are likewise becoming dark and sturdy looking.

These birds are now the definition of alert but are still totally dependent on my proximity for their sense of well-being. Many birds—for example, birds of prey and songbirds—typically have parents that leave their young for extended periods of time while they forage for food. The young of such birds are perfectly content to be left alone. Gallinaceous, ground-dwelling, precocial species, however, such as quail, pheasants, and turkeys, are born with the ability to walk and to feed themselves. Consequently it is unnatural for any of these young to be separated from their parent and, correspondingly, these young wild turkeys are made very unhappy in my absence.

I notice that as time goes by, we are developing a more complicated relationship. I sense that they are hungry for, or at least sensitive to, any communication from me. The slightest vocalization from me can now produce profound reactions, and I am learning gradually what is appropriate and what is not. It is as though we are becoming closer as time permits us to know each other better.

POULT AT TEN WEEKS.

Part III

June 13, Thursday

At daylight I release the turkeys into the pen from their snake-proof enclosure. Bright Eyes, the smallest by far, with unusually large eyes and a crooked left toe, is not altogether well, and after eating several crickets, refuses any more later in the day. She seems sluggish. I wonder if she is getting chilled at night.

After lunch I finally get up my nerve to take the turkeys for an extended walk outside, the first since the incident with the hawk. I have been very nervous about this, although I know it is more frightening for me than for them.

I begin by coaxing five through the gate, hoping to experiment with a small number. This does not work. They are torn between following me and staying with the group. I have to let out the whole group and head out up the old field, hoping for the best.

They all follow enthusiastically as I traverse from one tree to the next and wait in the shade until the assembly is complete. They seem somewhat cautious about all of this but neither confused nor afraid. They immediately set about foraging, hunting, and cautiously examining strange objects like longleaf pinecones. We make a brief foray out through the field and back to the pen and, with the enticing aid of the cricket cage, file in as pretty as you please. This weekend we will go for a more extended walk, in the cooler hours of the day. Several seem very hot upon our return and hold their wings and back feathers out. Most are panting as well. I am worried about Bright Eyes—she is eating and watering but not taking crickets or fresh greens. I have always favored her with extra crickets, and she has never before refused.

June 14, Friday

I let the poults out of their snake-proof cage. They are excited and spend much time flying about. Bright Eyes seems to feel somewhat better today, but I see her stagger a couple of times as though she is weak. She seems alert, however, and is eating well. I am looking forward to our next outing, probably tomorrow, although it makes me nervous. Yesterday I was reminded of how attached I am to these little birds, and how strong my feelings of responsibility are toward them.

The vitality and aggressive nature of these young wild turkeys constantly impresses me. They are exuberant and energetic but never belie an underlying seriousness about their lives. I see in them an awareness and a presence that remind me of how relatively dull my own senses are. They never fail to warn me of the slightest element of interest in our environment: a squirrel or bird in a nearby tree, a snake passing quietly nearby, or a hawk soaring at an altitude that is almost invisible to me.

Imprinting has caused them to look to me for information on the degree of danger associated with each situation or object. I am impressed with how they desperately want signals and communication from me, and how acute their attention to me is. The slightest yelp or purr from me can bring about the most profound behaviors: freezing, scattering, assembly, et cetera.

In response to all of this, I try to give appropriate signals and to show caution only when fear or caution is appropriate. For example, when a hawk is flying by or soaring overhead, I always freeze, watching the hawk and making a low cautious purr. This greatly impresses

the turkeys; they remain still and alert but not fearful. As soon as the hawk is out of sight, they resume normal behaviors. I am almost certain they instinctively differentiate between a soaring hawk and a soaring vulture, even at great heights. If this is true, it is a very sensitive differentiation.

June 15, Saturday

Today from the pen I heard the first attempt at a gobble as Claudia was starting the mower in the distance. The starter noise made the poults jump, and one could be heard attempting a spontaneous shock-induced gobble.

Later I observed the first real jake (young male) fight with serious sparring and spurring. When one finally submitted, the other spent considerable time pulling and twisting the skin of the defeated's head and neck. I want to walk with them, but I fear it is too hot. I photographed one jake in full strut this morning.

We go for our walk around four-thirty. This time we go much farther than before and have time to do some serious foraging. Many grasshoppers are captured as the birds pore through the grass and weeds together. Twenty pairs of little turkey feet make an interesting sound. I worry less now about losing any, as they are careful to stay close to me.

June 16, Sunday

By midmorning, the temperature is already hot—near 90 degrees—and the humidity is high. The yellow flies are the worst so far this summer.

Upon release from the snake-proof cage, all seem well and fly up and out immediately. I notice Bright Eyes stagger and then fall backward kicking and peeping. She looks as though she is having some sort of seizure. I pick her up, and she goes to sleep in my arms—she may be dying. In a few minutes she wants down. I put her down by the water, and she drinks and walks normally. A short time later I offer her crickets, which she eats enthusiastically. I don't know what to think.

I am having frustrating dreams nearly every night about these wild turkeys, and no matter where I am, I hear lost calls in my mind.

June 17, Monday

Last night I left the largest turkeys out of the snake-proof cage, hoping they would fly up to the roosting limbs hanging in the pen under the "dry roof." I stood among the roosting limbs, and they all readily flew up around me, but when I walked away, they flew down and tried to follow. So I just left them out and came back after dark. Most had flown up on a low limb in one of the corners. Two or three were walking about, and a couple were scattered off the ground here and there. Disappointed, I caught all of them and put them up on the roosting limbs, where they stayed all night, as far as I know. I now realize I will have to stay with them until after dark on the roost and then sneak away.

I am frequently reminded by these poults that for them there is apparently a whole language of color. Last week Claudia pulled up some old turnips and laid them by the pen for me to sort through and pick the tender greens for the poults. The poults regarded the turnips with alarm and suspicion. They would approach slowly with outstretched necks, delivering rapid alarm putts. This is common behavior with strange objects, but normally, after investigation, an inanimate object will be ignored. The turnips remained on the ground for several days as I gradually removed greens. The turkeys continued the alarm behavior off and on the entire time, and I finally concluded it was due to the bright color of the purple turnips.

One day I thoughtlessly walked into the pen with a bright blue T-shirt in my hand, and the turkeys began loud, coarse alarm yelping.

Claudia walks two miles each morning in half-mile laps, passing the turkey pen each lap. The turkeys, of course, know and accept her as family, but one day as I sat, I noticed that each time they saw her coming they became disturbed and began loud, coarse yelping. She was wearing a deep purple T-shirt. I noticed this behavior several other times when bright blue or purple was involved. I wonder if it is more than coincidence that aggressive mature spring gobblers have bright purple and blue on the sides of their heads.

Bright Eyes has had another seizure, losing all coordination and balance like before, but regaining both within a few minutes, resuming more or less normal behavior.

Now at six weeks, natal down is absent except for the head and neck. Some of the larger males are showing pink in the areas where the caruncles will appear on the neck. Most are showing bald spots on the back of the head. Larger juvenile flight feathers are now abundant in the pen as more continue to molt and fall, and one larger male (who I named Starker, with the crooked toe) has two new central tail feathers of the first-basic molt.

I've decided not to closely document feather development since this has been so well observed by Lovett Williams. I am more concerned with the instinctive and developmental aspects of behavior. I have been amazed since day one at how complete wild turkey behavior is from birth. Most of the obvious social, reproductive, defense, and feeding behaviors appear to be completely manifest insofar as physical strength will allow their display. Most learned behaviors appear to be in the form of specific adaptations to their particular environment. For example, the turkeys remember the locations of food sources and those where danger has occurred, such as the sites of predators' former positions. Their memory for these places is remarkable.

We finished the first fifty pounds of feed today. The man at the feed store was right—a few turkeys can eat fifty pounds of feed in a short time.

June 18, Tuesday

When I arrive at the pen this morning, I am confronted by a horrible sight. Three young turkeys have been killed and partially eaten. Only the heads appear to have been taken, with the exception of one thigh, which has been gnawed. I carefully examine the perimeter of the pen, checking for holes, but there are none. The door was closed and latched. No snake could have done this, not to mention that the poults are much too large for them now. It is as if these wild turkeys are providing some sort of vacuum into which all manner of predators are inexorably drawn. This $600 pen and my best efforts, it seems, are entirely transparent to them. I am outraged that these beautiful young birds are being snatched away seemingly at any predator's pleasure and overcome with a new empathy for the wild turkey hen and the incredible obstacles she and her young must face.

This reminds me of a friend living nearby who tried to raise some quail and discovered that weasels were entering the cages and killing them. He mentioned that only the heads were eaten. There is no hole anywhere larger than the one-inch mesh of the poultry wire. I can only imagine that it must have been a weasel, an animal I have never observed in over twenty years of living in this area.

Tonight, after our outing, I return all of the turkeys to the snakeproof pen. I have bought two large rat traps and baited them with meat from one of the dead poults. Bright Eyes was among the dead. I am very hurt about her in particular. She seemed to possess an extraordinary will to live. I am sorry I will not get to know her better.

June 19, Wednesday

This morning the traps are empty, but one has been sprung. I sit with the birds and drink my coffee. They seem subdued, indicating that they may have had a long night.

Late in the morning we go for a long, slow walk. I am worried that they might be less attentive to me on our walk, but they are very good and careful not to get too far away, apparently associating their safety totally with my presence. This week I want to reinforce these behaviors as much as possible by spending much time on foraging walks.

The gnats have gotten better. The yellow flies are bad at certain times, usually in late afternoon.

The young jakes are losing much more down on their heads, and a distinct blue cast may be observed on some. One jake has scabs on his neck from fighting. Fights are becoming more common but with even the victor acting submissive eventually. At this point the fighting appears to be lighthearted, almost recreational, and, for now, not sex related. Dewlaps on the upper necks are now becoming visible.

A pair of kingbirds is nesting out in the field in a large loblolly pine, thirty-five yards from the turkey pen. The nest is on the outer end of a large branch, thirty feet above the ground, and the male is presently standing guard on the power line nearby. He appears indifferent to us but may be seen in pursuit of the swallowtail kites that soar by several times each day.

Earlier Claudia and I were standing in the field when I heard a vaguely familiar cry. We looked up to see a bald eagle soaring overhead (maybe three hundred feet) accompanied by a little Mississippi kite. The odd companions eventually disappeared in overlapping sweeping circles to the west.

The turkeys look cautiously at a jet flying silently overhead, a silver speck probably above thirty thousand feet. They miss nothing.

June 20, Thursday

The turkeys are released from their snake-proof and weasel-proof cage in the A.M. All are fine. Traps were set the night before with raw turkey meat. No takers. Weasels do have a reputation for preferring to eat only what they have freshly killed. I don't know if there is any truth in this.

It is hot and humid today, so the yellow flies persist into midday. My elbows itch and burn. The turkeys think the flies are tasty little tidbits and are proficient at capturing them, even in midflight. A halictid bee shares my seat with me as I write—blue-green metallic brilliance.

Some of the larger turkeys, presumably jakes, are becoming more personable as they grow more familiar with me. A few even want to sit in my lap and sleep as they did when they were small. The smaller ones (hens, I suppose) are generally very affectionate, wanting to be held and touched.

Another productive walk, long and leisurely, although a couple of the hens seem stressed. Everything is so stimulating for them that it is hard to get them to forage casually in the heat of the day. They seem to be getting better at catching various insects and grasshoppers. Today I take many photos. While enjoying a gentle breeze, which makes things bearable, I watch a hen kill and eat a very large centipede. They must know if something is harmful or not, but it worries me. Discriminating among various insects, wild turkeys appear to be born entomologists.

Just before we arrive at the pen, something that I do not see flushes the turkeys like a covey of quail. I recoil but keep walking, and they quickly return and follow me into the pen. Their flush made an impressive noise.

In Herbert Stoddard's well-known study entitled *The Bobwhite Quail,* he refers to the peculiar sound created by the simultaneous flush of a startled covey of quail. Stoddard describes the phenomenon as a "thunderous rise" and as being "disconcerting." Further, he states that the behavior is reserved for "occasions when they are being flushed by enemies." At other times, for example, when the covey flies up on the roost, no such sound is produced. It is a startling event and would be distracting or even frightening for any potential predator. The survival advantages are obvious.

If quail flushing can be described as thunderous, then a flock of wild turkeys being flushed by a predator could only be described as explosive. Wild turkeys are large, heavy birds and even in normal flight they create a great deal of wing noise. But there is nothing like the sound of their panic flush. It is a real shock to experience at close range. It would be interesting to see a slow-motion film that demonstrated the mechanics of this phenomenon.

We observed a scissor-tailed flycatcher today, not far from the cabin. Twenty years have passed since my last Florida sighting, on Alligator Point, in Franklin County.

June 22, Saturday

Because of wild turkeys' secretive nature, a considerable mythology of misunderstanding has grown up around them to help us compensate for our ignorance. One particularly annoying belief concerns the wild turkey's difficulty negotiating fences and the presumption that this difficulty indicates a lack of intelligence.

These young wild turkeys recognize perfectly that a wire barrier limits their explorations. They never try to walk through the wire of the pen, and even in flight they will always avoid contact unless they are in a panic, and then, understandably, all bets are off.

Young wild turkeys are peculiar in that they have a predisposition to squeeze and force their way into tight places. As I sit against a tree, invariably one or more poults will wedge themselves tightly in the void between my lower back and the trunk of the tree. Similarly, others will find any space left under my knees and snuggle in for a warm nap. I must be careful when getting up not to injure anyone. Small mammals frequently enjoy this type of snuggling but, in my experience, not many birds.

Further, wild turkeys have thick, glossy, smooth feathers that, when compared to other birds, could be considered almost armored, and the ratio of head size to body size may be much greater than in almost any North American bird. I frequently observe that rather than going around a thicket of grass or shrubs, they are perfectly suited to enter and wedge their way through the thickest vegetation with their heads. The vegetation parts, and the glossy plumage allows the birds to slide silently and effortlessly through.

Unfortunately, when a wild turkey encounters a woven wire fence, it is generally shrouded in weeds and grasses, which are normally supposed to provide an avenue of escape. Wild turkeys are occasionally trapped and killed by dogs or other predators while trying to wedge their way through a fence. They are merely exercising a behavior that under normal circumstances has great survival value.

Another absurd notion is that in a rainstorm, young turkeys will stand with their bills up in the air and drown. Because wild turkeys are relatively large, it is difficult for them to find perfectly dry shelter in the wild. Besides entering thick vegetation and seeking out the natural "rain shadow" that exists under trees, they make their overhead silhouette as small as possible. With head up, neck raised, body erect, and tail down, the small amount of turkey that is exposed to the rain keeps the rest relatively dry. I refer to it as their rain posture.

Young turkeys, of course, have more difficulty shedding rain, and without cover may easily become chilled and die. They do not drown. Domestic turkey poults are particularly intolerant of being chilled. The person who sits and watches as his young birds die in the rain is probably the one whose intellect should be in question.

At night, I place the feeder in the snake-proof cage, and the birds fly up on the open top and drop down inside. I usually have to pick up a few and help them in. Some find this annoying; a few seem to appreciate the help. I suppose it's the memory of the brooder, but the confines of the snake-proof cage have a calming effect on the turkeys, and they soon begin to relax and lie around after entering.

There is more third-molt or first-basic plumage now. Central tail feathers, tail coverts, and feathers of the lower back and rump are beginning to show on many individuals. Interestingly, this development is not necessarily confined to the larger birds. One of the smaller hens is very advanced. At this stage, one might say that from a distance they appear to be about half of their adult size, standing between eighteen and twenty-four inches tall.

Yellow flies are not unbearable today—there is a gentle breeze. A cuckoo is nesting about seven feet above the ground in a young loblolly pine, just below the kingbird nest.

June 23, Sunday

The turkey who I call Putt Putt has not been doing well. I recognize her because she is particularly small, rather dark, and more vocal than any of the others, and often wants to sit in my lap. She tends to breathe through her slightly open bill, and yesterday she seemed to be having difficulty breathing. Judging by her general appearance and the brightness of her eyes, she may have a physiological problem rather than an infection. She "pips" or coughs occasionally and adjusts her neck as if there might be an obstruction or possibly a congenital defect. Today, however, she appears improved and is not struggling to breathe.

Maybe exercise will do Putt Putt some good. We leave the pen early and walk leisurely or sit for several hours. The poults are becoming more aggressive and range farther from me now (up to thirty yards) but never let me out of their sight or hearing. In their small world of seeds and grasshoppers I must loom like a mountain. So even when they have wandered into thick cover, I know they are aware of my whereabouts. And after a minute or two, they suddenly come on the run, with raised heads, to my side.

The old field and surrounding hammocks, bay swamps, and creeks will for a time be the center of our home range, the nucleus around which our lives will orbit. These wild turkeys have been born with the keys to unlock a bounty that still resides in this tired, worn-out piece of flatwoods. It is their birthright and its hidden assets are their legacy.

Deposited by successive advancing and retreating shallow seas, these ancient sand dunes, muddy bays, and barrier islands have been left stranded and tormented for millennia by meandering creeks and rivers. The field exists as an elevated finger, perhaps an old dune ridge, that projects north to south from a large expanse of poorly drained coastal lowlands: titi and cypress swamps, bayheads, and pine flatwoods. This bony little finger, less than a mile long and barely a quarter wide, was once a classic longleaf pine, wiregrass, and palmetto flatwoods. Bordered on the east and west by small hardwood drainages and on the south by Mill Creek, the Sopchoppy River, and their accompanying hardwood hammocks, these ancient virgin forests once reverberated with the sound of ivory-billed, and red-cockaded woodpeckers. Wolves and panthers prowled the margins of the hammocks as flocks of Carolina parakeets shrieked from the tops of fruiting tupelo trees. Occasionally, small whispering groups of native American hunters would camp temporarily near a cool branch as they pursued the abundant deer, wild turkey, and small game that traversed this ecologically diverse area. This land was once powerful and majestic; for tens of thousands of years it stood as a noble monument to the sublime grandeur of wilderness.

Then the white man came, and in only a couple of hundred years everything in the picture above was dead or displaced. This incredible wealth was turned into the ground and used to grow a generation of corn, eventually leaving the sandy soil in ruin.

First it was turpentine extracted from longleaf pine. Grimacing heart-pine stumps scarred with "cat faces" stand or lie everywhere in the wooded land surrounding the field. Then came the water-driven sawmills, and these ancient heart-pine logs became the strong wooden back of America's railroads. After the land had been cleared, mules and oxen pulled the stumps and turned under twelve inches of rich humus that had taken over ten thousand years to accumulate on these old sand ridges. In a single generation of corn and watermelons, the exposed sandy soil surrendered the last vestiges of its original bounty. By 1900, the land exhausted, the settlers left, except for a few determined and persistent individuals. Mr. Bert confessed to me as he sold me a parcel of his old farm, "This land won't even grow grass." Too depleted for agricultural crops, the soil could not support pasture grass for his few cattle.

Twenty years ago, I could stand and look north from the narrow hammock along Mill Creek to the national forest one-half mile away. The pasture was dotted with a few remnant old longleaf pines and a few patches of broom grass and blackberry. Ironically, though Mr. Bert's heirs logged off the scattered remaining old trees in the pasture, today few people would even recognize this land as having been a cornfield or pasture. In twenty years, young longleaf and invasive loblolly pines have come up everywhere in the old field, and each has created a refuge that has permitted a relatively rich variety of vegetation to establish a foothold. Species that long ago abandoned this land are now gradually reclaiming their territory. Wildlife, although still not abundant, is slowly beginning to reappear.

The turkeys and I forage beneath the young pines. Their low shading branches have formed an oasis of shade and moisture for plants, animals, and insects. The bounty that may be found living in these small areas is amazing. The turkeys miss very little in their explorations. All manner of grasshoppers are taken, but the larger ones are still regarded with caution. The enormous lubber grasshopper, known locally as Georgia thumper, is ignored completely. All spiders are regarded with caution, but most are killed and eaten. Flies of all sorts including deer flies and yellow flies are stalked, like a cat stalks a bird, and seized.

As a red-shouldered hawk screams and soars about the field, we practice being very still and hiding under the boughs and cover of a young pine. Three levels of vocalizations regarding distant soaring aerial predators have been taught to me by the turkeys and then reinforced in them by me. The first level of caution is represented by a lazy nasal whine, which serves to gain everyone's attention but is not alarming. Next, an ascending purr will bring about various cautionary behaviors like freezing or squatting and frequently serves as a signal to assemble and be still. If danger seems imminent, this signal will cause the turkeys to dive under the cover of a nearby bush. All of this is dependent on the inflection of the purr and the accompanying visual stimulus—hawk, kite, vulture, et cetera. All of which they seem to be able to differentiate. A raptor in straight flight is always more disturbing than one that is soaring.

After the turkeys have reacted to the alarm and are motionless, a low, breathy, voiceless hiss will bring about absolute silence and stillness for several minutes or until the hawk is out of sight. Then, gradually, the residual trilling and purring will resume along with normal foraging behavior. I have to be very careful what I say. I have inadvertently caused a couple of panics.

It is my intention to avoid using my human voice. When on a rare occasion I do, they tend to ignore the indiscretion as though it is some peculiar idiosyncrasy I alone possess. They have begun to find that I am odd.

June 24, Monday

Their appearance continues to change, making individual distinctions hard to maintain. All but a few birds are showing first-basic tail feathers. Their heads are becoming increasingly sparse, showing more blue, with pink caruncles on the young males. The heads of a couple of the small hens are still sparsely covered in natal down, Putt Putt being one of these. Some of the larger males are showing an orange cast in their tarsal scales. Dark primaries with white bars can be seen hanging below the closed wing. Many backs and rumps are showing the first dark feathers of the first-basic molt, which contrast sharply with the previous pale juvenile plumage.

The turkeys are beginning their seventh week of life. Their daily foraging appears to be providing them with much animal protein in the form of insects, and I continue to add fresh kale, sorrel, and turnip greens twice a day and occasionally crickets to their diet. Overall, they appear to be in extremely good condition, but I have no real frame of reference on this. They are consuming between three and four pounds of commercial turkey starter per day, in addition to the food obtained on our walks. Putt Putt still has some sort of breathing difficulty and occasionally coughs or pips. She is no worse than before and perhaps may have improved since the day before yesterday. She did just fine on our lengthy walk yesterday, and I even saw her kill and eat a very large katydid.

We enjoy a long walk through the field and surrounding woods. Both the turkeys and I are beginning to relax and consider our outings to be safe and routine. I am no longer counting heads each time we stop at a different location and I now have complete confidence in them. At one point I even tried to test their awareness by moving far ahead and hiding, but they all somehow knew exactly where I was and walked casually to my position. Anyone who has attempted to study turkeys in the wild has encountered the great difficulty of remaining undiscovered by these sensitive birds. As the turkeys grow and become more sturdy, my apprehensions about their health and safety lessen each day.

As I had hoped, the turkeys' behavior is, I believe, relatively unaffected by my presence on foraging walks. They are accumulating knowledge and skills each day that suggest to me that they are becoming real wild turkeys and not pen-raised poultry.

June 25, Tuesday

Today it is very hot, and Putt Putt is not well. We walk about seventy-five yards, and she falls down. I move ahead with the others to see if she will come or at least call. Nothing. She has given up. I carry her the rest of the way, and we return after only an hour or so and sit for a while. We are always much closer after a foraging walk.

June 26, Wednesday

The rain breaks around one-thirty. Leaving Putt Putt behind, sick and sleeping in the snake-proof cage, we set off to forage through the old field. It is cloudy and cool, so we keep moving, expanding our range, heading up toward the national forest. The turkeys never fail to warn me with staccato putting and long craning necks when they encounter anything unusual. Sometimes it's an odd stick, an old piece of glass, or an unusually large grasshopper. This afternoon it's a rattlesnake. As soon as I see him, I give the alarm purr and quickly move away. I don't want to take any chances, although I hope I am not depriving them of the opportunity to learn an important lesson. Later, they repeat their alarm behavior, but this time it is an irritated black racer, shaking his tail and spreading his head—this is perfect. I begin by giving the alarm purr, but this time I tap on the angry snake's tail with my foot, hoping he will dash off, startling the turkeys, who by this time have all gathered around to take a close look. Instead, he grows more aggressive, rears up like a cobra, and makes a big lashing strike at my leg. The turkeys are appalled, so I give several loud alarm putts and run a few feet away repeating the putts. Then I quickly move about thirty yards away, and the turkeys all take off on a run with heads held as high as possible until they reach my side. They then quickly settle back to typical foraging behavior. They appear much less respectful of the racer than of the rattlesnake.

Later, it begins to shower again, so we forage our way to the pen, where I coax them back in with a few crickets. Resting under the dry roof, they sleep and preen as I write these field notes. A wild turkey sleeps on my shoulder, one is sitting on my lap, and the rest are scattered around on the ground or above me on the roosting limbs. I am surrounded by a pleasant, warm bird scent, and their preening and constant trills combine to make a comforting sound as thunder rumbles in the distance. Flakes from feather sheaths rain around me like a light snowfall.

Putt Putt is unresponsive, uninterested in either food or water. She will probably not last through the night. Although not knowing for sure, I still don't believe she has a fever or an infection, but rather some mechanical problem. She wastes away.

June 27, Thursday

When I let the turkeys out of the snake-proof cage in the morning, I find that Putt Putt has died in the night in the same position in which I left her. I will miss her.

Rain again threatens, but we are lucky—storms move toward the north on either side of us. Occasionally, we see the sun, and the temperature is relatively cool. The turkeys are sun hungry and immediately begin to lie down and stretch out when it shines. The walk is long and deliberate, covering new and interesting territory. Much of the time, I let them lead the way. As the turkeys walk some distance ahead in the brightness of the open field, I notice that I can still tell the two family groups apart. Clutch #2 is still slightly darker. Clutch #1 is overall slightly larger.

Walking down an old sandy, abandoned roadbed that has become dim and overgrown, I remember that we saw a resident wild turkey hen feeding here yesterday. Looking for her tracks in the sand, I notice our own tracks, here where I have seen resident wild turkey tracks many times before. As I watch fresh tracks being made, I have a strange sensation, as though I am witnessing something special. Anyone who spends much time on the land will admit that a wild turkey track, when recognized, never fails to be intriguing. These fresh tracks are large enough to be easily identified as wild turkey tracks and not those of crows or some other large bird.

There is a rather tall (three feet) species of penstemon, commonly called beardtongue, that grows abundantly in the old field and these open pine woods. It makes a particularly showy display in the northern end of the field near the national forest. I was struck today by the image of these wild turkeys feeding and foraging through the open, white-flowered terrain. It was obvious that the turkeys belong in this environment and that they are very much a part of all this, a perfect fit.

I always move as slowly and as quietly as I can when we are foraging, in an attempt to keep their experience as unaffected by my own as possible. Ironically, I notice that my movements are very similar to those of a hunter. I am alert and slightly nervous, in a state of constant expectation. We are anticipating rattlesnakes and grasshoppers. Today, we find only grasshoppers.

The turkeys seem very close to me today—a strange, almost physical attachment. The young male I have come to call Little Friend is a constant fixture by my side, on my lap, or on my shoulder. As we browse, I can frequently hear a vocalization that seems to be reserved primarily for me. It is a voiceless, nasal sound approximating *shuuck, shuuck, shuuck.* This sound they always make when passing near or when I am touching them. Other vocalizations are expressed directly to me during interaction, but those sounds are also shared with other turkeys. I suspect it could be associated with deference or submission, but I prefer to think it's because they like me.

Now that Putt Putt is gone, I think all the turkeys are large enough to be roosting on the limbs provided in the pen. I am going to proceed, assuming the three losses to weasels were due to the fact that the turkeys had roosted on or near the ground. Removing the cage makes the pen much more pleasant and attractive.

I continue feeding them fresh greens, usually two or more times daily, commercial turkey starter, and two hundred crickets over a couple of days as treats and inducements, particularly when getting in and out of the pen. It is difficult to tell how much food they get on our walks; they are almost continuously eating something. I notice that in the evenings, after a walk, they are ambivalent about eating crickets in the pen. When crickets are fed in the pen at other times, a great frenzy of cricket chasing occurs.

While foraging through the fields and woods, we frequently spread out, forming a sort of skirmish line, side by side, a wave of wild turkeys. Insects such as moths, grasshoppers, and butterflies all flush before us. In this way, insects that hop or fly many feet often land directly in front of another turkey, and each turkey is always covering fresh ground. It is obviously a feeding strategy that wild turkeys are naturally prone to employ.

June 28, Friday

The turkeys spend their first night out of the snake-proof cage in ten days. Checking on them several times during the night, I make sure all are still up on the roosting limbs. Everyone does fine. I am certain that I have been overly cautious.

In spite of all the days we have spent together I never cease to be amazed by the behavior and appearance of these wild turkeys. It's as if I cannot quite take it all in. There is something about them that is too much for me to comprehend, and they become more astounding every day.

Since Putt Putt died, I am, for the first time, without any unhealthy or underdeveloped birds. To date, all of the individuals who have died of disease appear to have had congenital or inherent developmental problems. I don't believe we have had any type of viral or bacterial infection, although I cannot be absolutely sure of this.

Of the original twenty-three hatchlings, I have lost five to predation and two to degenerative physical ailments. I assume that in the wild these figures would be much higher.

June 29, Saturday

The turkeys did very well once again on their roost. I checked on them only twice, shortly after dark and again about 12:30 A.M.

The morning becomes hot early, with only an occasional breeze, and our walk is very slow. As we forage from one shady area to the next, I sit and let the turkeys browse around me. Some immediately begin panting and want to sit or lie around. The yellow flies are bothersome for all of us.

It is just too hot and still, so we begin to head back. After entering the pen, I notice one hen is not at the feeders. She appears weak, with drooping wings and diarrhea; I watch her as she continually tries to swallow. I think she may have been poisoned somehow.

An hour or so later she looks improved but still weak. I thought for a time that she was going to die, but by night she is apparently doing fine. She later has no difficulty flying up on the roost with the others.

June 30, Sunday

The sick one is better this morning, and I have a little trouble picking her out. She is wary today, as if holding me somehow responsible for her infirmity, probably as a result of handling her while she was very sick. This is the one who was pecked by the others when a few days old and had to be separated. She is one of the dark ones, relatively small with the middle toe on her left foot turning inward. From here on, I will call her Spooky. She is still a little weak today and sleeping more than the others. The afternoon is terribly hot and very humid, so I choose not to go for a walk—being left behind might be as stressful for her as walking in the heat. Also, I worry that her illness may have been something like heatstroke. As all of the birds became stressed yesterday in a heat in excess of 100 degrees, I'm not going to take a chance.

I spend most of the day with the turkeys in their pen, staying close and relaxing. This kind of time is well spent, it seems to me, and serves to bring us all closer together. I want to maintain this closeness as long as possible.

The turkeys react differently to my touch. A few seem to like being touched or stroked. Some are at first cautious of my hand but then assume a submissive sitting position and apparently enjoy the attention. Often they will close their eyes and fall fast asleep. Certain individuals do not want to be handled and will always move away from my hand when I reach for them. This behavior does not seem to be related to fear, however, as some who tolerate my touch the least have a greater need to be close and will find some way to have contact with me. Starker, one of the larger males who I can identify readily, wants to be sitting on me or next to me on the ground. He will snuggle in as close as possible, but invariably when I reach, he will move away, returning to my lap or side as soon as my attention is diverted. Several of the others act in a similar manner.

It occurs to me that wild turkeys have no means of grasping or holding. They never use their feet to grasp objects or food, as do many other birds. Any grasping done with their bills is only associated with fighting and aggression. It stands to reason that a grasping hand would be biologically unnatural for them and would be approximated in nature only when being captured by a predator. I have learned to be content with the proximity of these wild turkeys and experience their affection in that way.

I find myself occasionally using this word "affection" in describing the birds' behavior. That would bother some animal behaviorists. Perhaps affection in wild turkeys is something more akin to the security of flocking or herding behavior in socially organized animals and the comfort that close proximity affords any young animal. It could be our own arrogance, however, that causes us to believe that the human experience of affection is somehow more profound than that found in other species. In any case, I choose to perceive my experience with these wild turkeys as one of genuine affection. I have imprinted and raised many different species of animals, from small rodents to deer, and have experienced what I consider to be unconditional affection from the smallest to the largest. It is, however, easier for us to identify the attributes that we associate with affection in mammals. They express "affectionate" behavior just as humans and other primates do. Birds generally lack the equipment to display affection as overtly as mammals. Nevertheless, I believe that the wild turkeys' experience of affection is very well developed and is a significant part of their social environment.

July 2, Tuesday

As we forage up toward the forest on the old roadbed, I notice a small circular patch of thick grass that has been crushed, as if a small deer has bedded down here. I slow down to investigate, the turkeys following close behind. They are catching up after browsing in a patch of blackberries. I take another step in the thick, dark green grass, and a very large rattlesnake suddenly recoils from my foot. She makes a high coil, towering over the knee-high grass, and proceeds to buzz and hiss loudly—she is furious. I give a legitimate and heartfelt alarm purr, and the turkeys explode into flight, putting and running to a pile of rotting pine logs thirty feet away. The logs are probably where the snake has been living, but she is out here now, and I am proud of the poults' reaction.

I turn around after briefly examining the outraged diamondback and head back down the roadbed yelping softly with intermittent alarm purrs. The turkeys begin leaving the log pile, and all eventually join me, giving the snake a wide berth as we head up through the field foraging. They follow, staying closer as I move more cautiously, listening to the sound of rattling fade into the distance. That was a very big snake—well over five feet. I am almost certain that I actually touched her head with my foot.

July 3, Wednesday

The turkeys' appearance continues to change daily. With less down on their heads and first-basic longer tails, they are beginning to look like miniature adults in form. Adding to this effect are legs that are becoming long and powerful. An obvious lack of awkwardness in young wild turkeys brings to mind the strong appearance of graceful young athletes. Their heads now show little natal down. The yellow down has molted away on a few individuals, leaving the darker brown down and giving a blotchy look to their heads. This is particularly apparent on the darker turkeys from clutch #2. The lighter ones from clutch #1 have molted more cleanly on their heads and have a neat pale blue appearance by comparison.

Two pairs of central tail feathers, of the third or first-basic molt, can be seen on almost all of the turkeys, with the exception of one or two who are well on their way. Dark feathers of the third molt are coming in well on upper and lower backs in linear order. Emerging contour feathers on the sides of the breasts are also apparent. Two or three greater secondary coverts may be seen on the wings and have some of the beautiful purple-bronze iridescence common to all adult wild turkeys.

Feathers of the first-basic molt, in addition to having iridescence, lack the rounded tips of juvenile feathers. First-basic feathers tend to have square or flat tips as seen on adult wild turkeys.

The young jakes are showing more development and swelling in their neck caruncles. The large central and two lateral caruncles on the lower neck are also beginning to show "color." While I was handling a jake with a bright red caruncle, it slowly began to turn pale. I thought it was an injury at first. This is the first evidence of skin-color change in response to excitement that I've observed in these birds.

Fighting still occurs among the poults, but I am seeing less serious fighting and more tendency toward mutual submission. It is as if they have already discovered that intense fights are painful and tiring. Perhaps they have already begun to know who will be dominant. Strutting is common and often brings about submissive behavior in the hens. However, even the largest jakes will take turns being submissive, even to the smallest hens. It is amusing to see the largest jake crouched in a submissive pose, prostrate, with neck outstretched, eyes closed, and the smallest hen standing over him periodically pecking him on the head. Minutes later he is up, strutting around being the bad turkey, looking for trouble.

It begins raining in the afternoon. Watching from the porch through the hammock, it looks as though the poults are under the dry roof. When they see me on the porch, they come out into the rain to try to reach me. I sit quietly and write, and they go back under. They are not at all waterproof like ducks but can, with the exception of their heads and backs, remain remarkably dry. I no longer worry about them getting wet.

July 5, Friday

It has been gently raining off and on all day. I sit with the poults for a while, but we are overcome with the desire to be out—we go for a walk in the rain. The turkeys seem to remain relatively dry as we go from one young pine to the next, wandering up into the field in a light drizzle, seeking refuge in the rain shadow that exists under most young pines. Often these areas are absolutely dry and afford a very cozy spot to rest when the rain periodically falls harder. These birds are innately aware of this rain shadow phenomenon. After thoroughly browsing such an area, we dart to the next dry refuge, shaking the accumulated water off our backs. They seem to be enjoying all of this and are particularly enthusiastic—the cool temperature is invigorating. We find that many grasshoppers and other insects have also sought out these dryer areas. Gradually, we move up through the field, stopping now and then to relax and watch the gentle rain fall around us.

Eventually, the showers wane, and we resume normal browsing. At the upper end of the field, as I sit, the turkeys work their way twenty or thirty yards back toward the south. Frequently, as we move, I will stop and sit while they browse in a radius around me. The sun is shining on the wet land, it is still cool, and in all it is a beautiful scene. With the turkeys almost completely out of sight, I suddenly move directly north. I stop seventy-five yards from them in a blackberry patch that exists as an open area in an otherwise thick stand of pines mixed with an understory of large wax myrtles and deer berry. The turkeys begin to softly lost call as they realize I am no longer within their sight or hearing. I give a very soft double yelp and hear a flutter. Suddenly the air and trees are filled with wild turkeys, flying over and through. With a great swoosh of strong wings, sixteen wild turkeys pitch in all around me with loud staccato putts and coarse yelps. They immediately begin enthusiastically harvesting blackberries. It is a spectacular sight, one I know I will relive in my mind for years to come.

In the last few weeks, I have noticed some interesting aspects of social behavior in these wild turkeys that seem to be centered around two separate instincts: one, to be with the parent; and the other, to be with the group. Of these two forces the stronger pull within the individual is apparently to the flock, not the parent. For a long time this disturbed me and was confusing. I would see an individual turkey, left by the others as they fed away in a group, become anxious, torn between staying at my side or running to catch up with the flock. Invariably, the lone bird would eventually go running in a confused panic to the group. This in spite, sometimes, of my reassuring vocalizations. I interpreted this as a type of rejection and assumed it was because the turkeys were not totally imprinted on me. I now suspect that this is not the case. Konrad Lorenz noticed a similar stratification among brooding graylag geese.

Flocking behavior appears to break down into two levels. The individual is bound to the flock as his primary orientation. The flock as a whole is then oriented to the parent. After much deliberation, I now believe that this has great survival value. If your own children were to become lost, you would want them to stay together at all costs. There is safety in numbers, and a group is easier to find than many lost individuals.

A lost young wild turkey will go to any turkey he sees or hears, but if given a choice, he will always join a group. The group as a whole will then faithfully seek the parent. And a whole flock of wild turkeys making lost calls can be heard for a great distance.

We continue our walk until late in the evening. Insects are abundant. We encounter no snakes and, with the exception of a cottontail rabbit, we see no other large animals. Earlier, a great flock of purple grackles passed to our south, and upon our return we find two trapped in the open pen. I am afraid this will scare the turkeys and prevent them from reentering the pen, but the turkeys are unimpressed and, with the aid of a few crickets, file in orderly. We walk to the back of the pen, and the confused grackles fly out the open door.

As night begins to fall, I fill the turkeys' feeders and then stay with them until they fly up on the roost. The roosting limbs are at about eye level, so I stand among the limbs, and all soon fly up around me. After a bit of confusion about the best roosting spots and exercises in how many turkeys can sit on the head of a man, they all settle down and begin to sleep, some with heads tucked under wings, some with heads hanging. Gradually, along with the daylight, the soft purrs and trills subside, and I slip silently out of the pen in the darkness. The turkeys dream of fat, green grasshoppers and plump, ripe blackberries. I go dream about wild turkeys.

July 6, Saturday

As we sit in the pen waiting for the rain to pass, I hear a red-shouldered hawk calling loudly nearby. The turkeys seem a little indifferent, so I reinforce caution with a very soft alarm purr. They panic and flush; some hit the fence hard. I look around and see a fresh cut on one's head. The cut is small, near the nostrils on the area between the smooth bill and the snood. One other hen had a similar wire cut that has healed rather slowly, accompanied by a temporary deformity or hard swelling of the tissue in the area. I will no longer make any alarm sounds while the turkeys are in the pen.

From the pen, I look out and see two deer browsing in the open part of the field. At 150 yards or so, I can see that both are mature bucks with branching antlers in the velvet. They are quite reddish this time of year and contrast sharply with the lush green of the freshly watered field. I delay our walk in deference to the deer. We see deer tracks here regularly but not in great abundance. We rarely see mature bucks on this property.

Later, when the deer have moved off, we finally begin browsing up through the field. The temperature is pleasant. The sky is overcast, but the rain has passed. Heading toward the upper end of the field, we explore some new areas and find plenty of ripe blackberries and deer berries.

When any turkey shows interest in anything, I always try to investigate. Three turkeys are putting and pecking competitively in a clump of grass. I find that they have a large broken piece of a wild turkey egg. Seeing one of the poults peck off a small bit and swallow it, I pick up the pieces as they move on. Presumably, a resident wild turkey has nested somewhere nearby. A quarter mile north, I see several poults once again showing excitement over something. Investigating, I find another large piece of wild turkey egg, faded, but obviously from this year.

Later, as we head back by way of the old roadbed, I look ahead for fresh wild turkey tracks in the sand. I see a few deer tracks but no signs of resident wild turkeys. There are only a couple of sandy areas, so this is not a very representative sample of the activity in the area. I look down among the crowd of turkeys walking around me and see a freshly dropped tail feather from a mature resident wild turkey. It is fresh and unbroken. I pick it up, and all the turkeys gather around to examine it. Some want to gently peck, but most observe respectfully. All appear to be impressed at the sight of such a large feather. I bring the feather along, feeling the need to preserve it somehow. Perhaps some of these wild turkeys will live to have tails so profound.

While we are gradually foraging back toward home, two turkeys alarm putt. We see a black racer with milky, "shedding" eyes, but none of the turkeys want to commune. We move on.

Rain begins to fall just before dark, so I try to encourage them up on the roost before they get wet. As they settle down in a rather hard downpour, I notice they always seem to be pleased when I join them at roosting time. I enjoy the time as well, I must confess, although the mosquitoes can be a bother. I stay among the cozy, nodding group until after dark and then make a quiet dash for the cabin.

July 7, Sunday

By midmorning it has become extremely hot and humid. Yellow flies are scarce, however, and that helps prevent the day from being unbearable. Perhaps it will cloud over this afternoon, and we can go for a long walk.

Around noon, I quickly run up to the north property boundary. As I pass the old roadbed, I naturally think of the rattlesnake we encountered a few days before and walk the thirty-five yards north to the spot where we last saw her. We passed this way yesterday but did not go out of our way to find the snake. Knowing these snakes are somewhat territorial and thinking the rotten log pile by the old road a good candidate for a rattlesnake home, I begin peeking and poking around. Sure enough, there she is, lying up by the larger end of the logs. The large ends are the least rotten and afford secret places shaded by deer berry, wild azalea, grasses, and other plants that have grown up around the damp logs.

Already alerted to my intrusion, she ever so slowly moves back under the dark safety of the logs. I move in very close as her tail begins to enter the logs. I count thirteen rattles and notice that the tail swells abruptly into what is a very thick body. My life would be diminished if rattlesnakes were not in my world. Like grizzly bears, they are a part of wilderness that will not scamper off but will stand and look you dead in the eye.

As a matter of philosophy and respect, I never harm rattlesnakes, but I certainly recognize their lethal potential. I have always considered in fun that for every rattlesnake encountered in the wild and allowed to go relatively undisturbed, I build up "mystical points"— good herpetological karma—whatever, and that somehow these points act on my behalf if and when I am careless enough to tread dangerously close to a snake. I have had many remarkably close run-ins with rattlesnakes and gratefully have never been harmed. I like to think it is because I have a good standing among the great serpents.

However—I am concerned about this particular snake. She lives where people and animals I love dearly traverse almost daily. I feel she must go, even though a part of me loves knowing that she is here. She is situated in a place that will make it difficult to capture her. I am going to have to do something soon. I will think on this.

July 8, Monday

I join the turkeys at daylight, and we enjoy a morning that is relatively cool and overcast. Little Friend is very sick. He is lethargic and prefers to stand rather than sit; I have found that this is a bad sign. He is one of the dark ones from clutch #2 and has always been relatively large and healthy; I can only hope he has eaten something bad. I worry that he could have contracted some infection from secondary exposure to wild turkeys on our walks. Fowl pox is inevitable in young poults, but there is always the possibility of something worse. All of the others seem to feel particularly good today with the cooler weather. When we walk, Little Friend will have to stay behind. Perhaps he will recover inside the snake-proof cage, which is now just outside the pen. It is difficult to leave him.

The sun appears, and the temperature turns very hot. We move slowly but deliberately north, staying farther to the western side of the old field, and explore all new territory. While visiting the extreme northern part of the field bordering the national forest, in country we have never entered, we find a recently deceased gopher tortoise under a long-leaf pine. This area of the old field has grown up in thick long-leaf pine, water oak, persimmon, live oak, sparkleberry, deer berry, and abundant lowbush gallberry. Gallberries, although green, are readily eaten by the turkeys but not in great quantity.

We spend much time in shady thickets of wax myrtle and gall-berry, and judging by the abundant tracks and occasional beds, many deer have also sought refuge here. The turkeys suddenly startle—a red-

tailed hawk has alit somewhere nearby. I stand up to make my presence known, and he flies out of a neighboring pine. Hawks are constantly eyeing us, and I worry about attacks.

Later, a male bobwhite quail calls a few hundred yards to the north, while we are sitting under a spreading live oak with relatively thick undergrowth all around. I give a female quail assembly call, and he comes on the fly. He calls once again from fifty yards away. The turkeys are milling around under the live oak, and I hide by a bushy deer berry. Calling again, I see him moving in toward us through the grass. The turkeys spot the quail first, then the quail sees the turkeys. There is a brief moment of apparent recognition as the turkeys walk with curiosity toward their squat and distant relative. Suddenly everyone stops, as if not knowing how to respond to the little intruder. Disappointed, the quail skirts the inquisitive group, flies up in a nearby tree, and continues calling for another ten minutes. We move on.

Working our way across the northern end of the old field, browsing on ripe deer berries and blackberries, we begin to suffer from the intense heat. We arrive at the eastern edge of the old field, bordering a hammock that enshrouds a beautiful little limestone-bottom creek named Bert's Branch, which runs from a swampy area in the national forest south, joining Mill Creek just before it flows into the Sopchoppy River. The margin between the field and the creek is old mesic hardwood hammock. Hickory, laurel oak, water oak, live oak, swamp chestnut oak, holly, magnolia, dogwood, sparkleberry, yellow poplar, sweet bay, red bay, both upland and water tupelos, hazel alder, many wild azaleas (*Rhododendron canescens* and *R. serrulatum*), red maple, witch hazel, old-man's-beard (*Chionanthus*), gallberry, possum haw, palmetto, and many species of ericaceous shrubs all abound along these creeks. Ironwood (eastern hophornbeam) and bluebeech occur near the lower end of the branch. Needle palm, sable palm, and sable minor grow occasionally in areas close to the river.

The turkeys have never been to the branch. I have intentionally avoided the thick hardwoods, thinking that if something happened, it would be more difficult to get everyone reassembled in the thick cover adjoining the hammock. Further, the field affords much better browsing, of both insects and seed-bearing plants, than does the hammock. The turkeys have never encountered "live" water. Moving through an open wooded area that exists between the scrub of the field and the branch, I arrive at the edge of the stream with the turkeys following ten yards behind. Easing down a green, mossy embankment of a few feet that slopes to the creek below, I quietly come to rest by the edge of the water. The creek is about five feet wide here, with a gray, sandy bar a foot wide at my feet. The clear amber water is only a few inches deep, with a rather active current from all the recent rains. Mottled sunlight dances on the sandy bottom as mosquito fish dart in the flow. The sound of moving water echoes through the hammock, tumbling over a small rocky rapids above us, and then again over another one just below. The turkeys reach the top of the embankment, and all line up. Necks are outstretched, and nervous little yelps and putts can be heard from everyone. With mouths agape, they appear absolutely astonished. Very gradually, the boldest begin to move down the embankment. Some are hesitant to walk down the small hill and wait at the top. Dark metallic damselflies flit in the sunlight. Leopard frogs dive for the water as the turkeys cautiously, like a wave of feathered molasses, pour slowly over the embankment. They are mesmerized by the sight of so much moving water, like some great transparent serpent slowly moving through the dark forest. Gradually, some reach the branch and walk its edge. In spite of our long, hot walk, it is some time before anyone thinks of taking a drink. It is cool here, and surprisingly there are no annoying insects. Like a comforting friend, the creek surrounds the turkeys in quiet, dark secrecy, a refuge from the openness of the field and the heat and dryness of midday. Eventually, a couple of brave ones wade an inch or two into the edge of the water and drink, but very cautiously, as if only to sample this new water and not to drink deeply. Others seem to be examining interesting new plants and mushrooms that are abundant along these banks. All of the turkeys move slowly and deliberately, vocalizing faintly, admiring this wondrous new world. We will return here many times in the future. For now we must move back toward home, as a thunderstorm approaches from the southwest. The turkeys are slow to follow me back out into the hot buzzing world of the field. Eventually, they join me, running to my side. We carefully pass the home of the big rattlesnake and arrive at the pen just as rain begins to fall.

My excitement is dampened by the sight of Little Friend, who appears to be worse. I keep him separated from the others and leave him in the snake-proof cage. It is probably too late to avoid exposure to the others, but he may rest better if he avoids the confusion of the group. His coordination and equilibrium are not good, and his head droops. Surprisingly, he eats rather well, but he seems to have difficulty pecking. His eyes have a very peculiar look that I cannot describe. This could be an infection.

July 10, Wednesday

I fill Little Friend's waterer with dilute Terramycin. He barely hangs on. On the phone, a veterinarian friend suggests starting the others on Terramycin in their water. After driving straight to town and returning several hours later with more antibiotic, I discover that Little Friend died while I was gone. I start the other turkeys on one tablespoon of medicine per gallon of water. I am worried about Spooky. She seems weak and a likely candidate for illness. The others all appear to be normal.

Returning to the pen before dark, I put the turkeys to roost. The absence of Little Friend is conspicuous. Unfortunately, I now have a small wild turkey cemetery.

July 11, Thursday

The morning is hot and humid, but everyone is healthy and eager to get out. We make a wide loop, up by the big lone hickory tree in the field, where we see old deer rubs on a couple of saplings. Going slow, we sit and rest frequently.

Eventually, we make our way across the field and over to the spot on Bert's Branch that we visited earlier in the week. As we near the creek, the turkeys run ahead in anticipation. Clearly, they remember the spot and are still enchanted by the creek. As we spend time sitting and observing, each turkey seems to eventually take a turn carefully wading in the clear, flowing water. Today they all drink deeply.

We gradually begin working our way down the west bank of the creek. The turkeys have never spent this much time in a mature hardwood area, but they are very much at home, casually browsing on deer berries, various seeds, mushrooms, insects, and spiders. One of the smaller hens plucks a rather large, green anole from a deer berry bush, gives it a couple of brisk shakes, runs a few feet away from a jealous companion, and then swallows it. We are eating lizards! The turkeys are growing up. I am surprised by the lack of caution used with this large lizard. Perhaps they have already eaten green anoles without my having observed it.

We work our way to the edge of the hardwood hammock and the old field scrub, resting in a protected area of thick young hardwoods that overshadow a rich carpet of deer tongue, lichen, and hat pins. Moving a few yards farther out, we encounter an ancient spreading live oak that is surrounded by the thick young growth of the old field. We enter the protection of the live oak, and I immediately climb up into the canopy of the old tree. The turkeys all fly up around me. Having never been so high in such a great tree, they appear to observe the new perspective as a great revelation. Suddenly, there is loud protesting— a curious raccoon tries to join us. After much putting and jeering the rejected raccoon agrees to leave, and we resume meditative tree sitting.

Storms are coming. The turkeys are reluctant to leave the protective tree but do eventually, and we head for the safety of home.

July 12, Friday

We enjoy a long, productive walk, though the gnats are bothersome. It is very hot and humid, probably in the high 90s. As we examine some fresh deer tracks that seem unusually large, a cottontail rabbit jumps from under our feet and dashes away. The turkeys are very interested and seem to look to me for information. Confounded by their persistent solicitation, I shrug and say, "It's just a bunny." They eventually resume foraging but only after conveying what I perceive to be a certain dissatisfaction with my response. They consider me hopelessly obtuse.

We have encountered more broken wild turkey eggs. I wish I could find the nest site, but the broken eggs seem randomly scattered about the old field. Wild turkeys are very fond of all bird eggs—good calcium source, I suppose.

In *The Bobwhite Quail* (1931), Herb Stoddard mentions the wild turkey's apparent "fondness" for quail eggs. He reports on a mature gobbler in the act of destroying a hatching nest and apparently devouring four of the hatchling quail. He later suggests, however, that wild turkey predation on quail nests does not have a serious limiting effect on overall bobwhite populations. All bird eggshells found on the ground are readily eaten by these wild turkeys. We have encountered no quail nests.

The red-shouldered hawks, which are always present, came near again today. I gave a quiet alarm purr, and the turkeys all hid very well under a young spreading pine.

July 13, Saturday

The weather is still, humid, and unbearably hot. The turkeys all pant, so we wait until late in the day to walk and hope it will not be raining.

The turkeys all seem to be in good condition, so I discontinued the medication as of last night. Spooky still seems a little odd, but I think it is just the best she can do. She is more friendly now and seems to have forgiven me for her previous infirmity.

Growth continues to be rapid, and first-basic plumage is beginning to dominate the turkeys' appearance. When standing, their eye level now averages around twenty-six inches. All heads are very sparse of natal down. Swelling of the caruncles is apparent on all the young males. Rectrices, or tail feathers, are getting long and beautiful, with three or four pairs very well emerged. Tail coverts are likewise getting long. Juvenile contour feathers of the back, sides, and breast are generally being replaced by the darker feathers of the first-basic molt. Bronze, black-tipped, iridescent feathers are emerging on the back and are originating from the proximal area of the wing. Many first-basic primaries and secondaries can be seen emerging and radiating from the joint of the distal end of the radius and ulna. These contrast sharply in size and color with the juvenile wing plumage. The scales of the tarsi and feet have turned a rich, honey brown with a faint reddish deposition of pigment in each scale. In all, they are becoming handsome, strong-looking wild turkeys. If wild turkeys ever have an awkward age, I suppose this would be it, but they do not. I see only a remarkable grace that increases every day as this perfect form discovers its perfect function.

We go for a leisurely walk in the late afternoon. Storms threaten in the distance, and, after browsing the field, we work our way over to our favorite spot on Bert's Branch. Today, the turkeys discover all the overhanging limbs surrounding the creek and the interesting vantage points they provide. Considerable time is spent flying from tree to tree and limb to limb. These explorations seem to be confined to the understory trees overhanging the creek and do not involve the canopy. A turkey will find just the right spot overlooking the creek, sit down on a limb as if to roost, admire the view for a minute or two, and then fly to another interesting location. Each turkey is eventually joined by several others who, in turn, admire the view in leapfrog fashion. I quietly move up the creek, and all eventually follow, stopping occasionally to sample the deer berries here and there. Since it is distracting to the group when I pull something out of my pack to eat, I rely heavily on the same fruit that the turkeys feed on. But at least for now I leave the bugs to the birds.

We spend much of the day exploring down the creek, crossing over at one point, and then work back up the other side. Other wild turkeys are about. Like ghosts, they occasionally appear and disappear in the distance. We are being watched.

July 14, Sunday

The morning is hot and humid, so we spend some time sitting in the pen. The turkeys do not like my choice of shirts today and try to remove it—back to my uniform. I thought that a light brown would go unnoticed, but they want me in light blue.

Thunder rumbles at midday, and we have a heavy rain in midafternoon. The rain lets up around four, and we move up toward the forest. It is relatively cool and overcast, the land is wet and green, and the air is heavy with mist. Moving up the west side of the field, we browse on insects and most anything else. As we near the forest border, the land changes to old cut-over longleaf pine flatwoods with scrubby palmettos and small live oaks. The ground is sparsely covered with hat pins, lichens, bog grasses, and sedges. I look from a thicket, and thirty-five yards ahead I see the tawny body of a deer standing and staring in our direction. She is alert to our presence but undecided about who this might be. I stop still with several small water oaks separating us. The turkeys proceed past me, feeding, and approach the grassy clearing and the doe. She watches intently as the turkeys enter the open area. She bobs her head a couple of times, and her tail flits in response to the mosquitoes and gnats, which are rather bad today. Suddenly, one of the turkeys sees her and gives an alarm putt or two. Immediately, all heads go up, and a light chorus of cautionary putts ensues. To my surprise, the doe walks a few steps toward the turkeys, and inquisitively several of the turkeys likewise begin to approach her with necks raised high. Then, as if recognizing that no danger is at hand, the doe begins browsing and the turkeys become indifferent, although they choose gradually to return to me in the thicket.

I detected a distinct moment of recognition in the birds, as if a pre-existing set of criteria defining the deer had suddenly been satisfied. With no apparent experience necessary, they identify this large creature as a benevolent neighbor. With big ears, large tawny furred body, long face, and an intense stare, it could be said that the deer shares many superficial attributes with certain mammalian predators such as the coyote. Recently a coyote proved very disturbing to these turkeys even though he only passed by in the distance. It is clear that extremely specific information resides in these wild turkeys from birth. A few minutes later the doe wanders away, and I begin scratching a multitude of mosquito bites. I feel this encounter was a bit of a milestone for these young birds. They are gradually being introduced to all the inhabitants

with which they will share this land (although it was obvious that no real introduction was needed). I feel very good about that.

Shortly after encountering the deer, we happen upon an elderly box turtle, judging by the scarred and tattered condition of his carapace. An oddly protracted period of alarm putting follows in response to this clumsy little reptile. I move ahead, and the turkeys reluctantly stop jeering and join me. Turtles, it seems, are inherently more disturbing to wild turkeys than are deer. Perhaps they view a turtle as just a snake in a box.

We finish the walk by browsing on the abundant deer berries and notice that blackberries are getting scarce. Grasshoppers are plentiful and do not fly well after the rain, resulting in their easy capture. The large American bird grasshopper (*Schistocerca*) is abundant today and a prized catch.

July 15, Monday

The air is very humid, and we progress slowly in our outing, moving up the west side of the old field, cutting across and eventually entering Bert's Branch. The turkeys enter the branch and remind me of egrets as they hunt in the vegetation bordering the water. As the day is cloudy and humid, the mosquitoes force me to come up out of the creek bed. The turkeys respond by resuming tree-sitting activities above me in

the understory surrounding the creek. The process proceeds with a great deal of racket from flapping wings, snapping limbs, and excited vocalizations. Our recreation is interrupted by a noisy red-shouldered hawk in a tree seventy-five yards away that is being harassed by angry jays and a pair of great crested flycatchers. The turkeys rejoin me on the ground, and we browse slowly toward the field. We have to cut our walk short, heading for home in a light shower, as thunder and lightning threaten all around. I am out of crickets, but the turkeys choose to follow me into the pen as usual.

We sit for a while in the pen waiting on the rain. As I write, the turkeys all gather close around me, preening and sleeping. Every day the turkeys learn more about their environment and hone their survival skills. I try to perceive the minute details of their behavior and experience, but they are often too much for me. There is more going on with them every instant than I can possibly follow or comprehend. I am beginning to suspect that no matter how much time I spend with these birds, they will always remain a mystery to me. For now we will continue to share our lives, as much as time and necessity will permit, and I will continue to observe.

As with many animals, such as cats, deer, and even people, wild turkeys appear to have a well-developed sense of place, probably based on a feeling of well-being brought about by environmental conditions affording safety, shelter, a view of potential predators, and the like. In addition to these strategic attributes, a sense of place could also incorporate an element of aesthetic appreciation. Wild turkeys seem to have an aesthetic awareness of place and will want to spend time observing and just being in certain pleasing areas. After they identify a specific location as attractive and accommodating, that area is thereafter recognized and even anticipated. As we approach a favorite spot, the turkeys will often run ahead, as if the place itself satisfied some need. Upon entering the site, sitting, lounging, stretching, and other relaxing behaviors will invariably occur. I recognize in these places generally some subtle element that is attractive to me as well—a place to practice being.

July 17, Wednesday

We go for a pleasant walk in late afternoon after some heavy down-pours. Showers fall lightly as we travel through the field and up the old roadbed. I removed the big rattlesnake this morning after one of the showers had ended. Using a garden hoe, I gently lifted the great snake from the rotting logs where she lay peacefully coiled. Before she could become enraged, I had already lowered her thick serpentine form into a waiting ice chest. She began to rattle loudly just as I closed the lid and continued rattling intermittently all the way to the cabin. Tonight I will transport her to a more remote area of the forest. If it were just me, I would leave her and take my chances, but she repre-sented too much danger being this close. We all walk more comfort-ably past the log pile today, although I'm sure there are plenty of other rattlesnakes elsewhere. I hope they will continue to be shy and keep their distance. We will continue to be watchful.

People who handle poisonous snakes regularly always get bitten—it is axiomatic. Like all the rest, I thought for a time that I would be the exception and so held jobs while in college that required me to handle venomous reptiles every day. After a couple of years and sev-eral golden opportunities to sustain bites, it occurred to me that my days among the ranks of the great unbitten were numbered. And so I resolved generally not to put my hands on anything that could bring about their amputation or my death. In those days I had good equip-ment designed for handling dangerous snakes, but now I have noth-ing of the kind. I find, however, that when necessity dictates, a common garden hoe will serve as a snake hook of sorts and an ice chest works just fine for safe temporary housing and transportation. Now, only on rare occasions am I overcome with the desire to put my hands directly on the diamondback or the cottonmouth, the coral snake or the pygmy rattler. Often it is merely a matter of temperament—theirs and mine—some chemistry between us that deems our contact irre-sistible to me. But I have become sympathetic to the unnecessary trauma imposed on an extremely sensitive, aware, and wild creature. I am certain that they would consider my affections to be misplaced.

After flushing some quail on the northern end of the old field, we find a new entrance to Bert's Branch, but our stay is cut short as shadows begin to lengthen. We leisurely work our way back after a typical fourteen-hour day. Within the last two days, the blackberries have almost completely disappeared. Various species of grasses are developing now, and their seeds will help compensate for the loss of this valuable food source. I roost with the turkeys and then return to the cabin after dark.

July 18, Thursday

Rain falls for the third consecutive day. The turkeys remain on the roost, and I remain in bed. It stops around 9:00 A.M., and the sky is overcast but not threatening. The temperature is agreeable, and for the first time this summer there are no gnats. There are a few mosquitoes, of course, but they are not distracting. The turkeys seem subdued, and we feed slowly up through the field. I think they are sun hungry and would like to dust, but we have only dark clouds and wet sand. They are concentrating very heavily on seeds today for some reason. I also hear green pods snapping around me, as they eat the creeping *Crotalaria,* known commonly as one of the rabbit bells (*C. sagittalis*) that grow abundantly in these pine woods. Some species of crotalaria have a reputation for being poisonous to grazing livestock, but this particular species has a green pod that smells as fresh and sweet as any English pea. The wild turkeys are extremely fond of them. I find myself nibbling on one occasionally as well.

The birds become interested in two or three limby young longleaf pines growing on the edge of a live oak thicket. I sit down and watch as they involve themselves in what I now call limbing behavior. This consists of sitting and flying from limb to limb, periodically relaxing and preening. It is a noisy process with much flapping about and vocalization. This behavior appears almost recreational but may also precede a resting period during the day. In years past, I have observed wild turkeys engaged in this curious activity and wondered what could possibly be going on. I watch for thirty minutes or so and then begin walking away. The turkeys eventually join me by flying the fifty or sixty yards that separate us. We find a new blackberry patch that still has ripe berries in great quantity. We all load up.

Later, we are up near the forest border where the ground is low and acidic, sparsely covered in bog button, hat pins, yellow-eyed grass, running oak, lichen, and longleaf pine. The turkeys suddenly begin alarm putting just behind me, which is always disconcerting, and I realize that they have found a beautiful scarlet snake about fourteen inches long. They are very interested, putt lightly, and take turns examining the snake closely. The shy scarlet snake moves along, and so do we.

In addition to the wild turkeys' curiosity with things potentially edible or dangerous, which has an obvious survival role, an interest in things that do not facilitate survival directly occupies much of their time and attention.

Young wild turkeys are obsessively drawn to objects that are unusual or that contrast sharply with their surroundings. In this way, all manner of strange artifacts are brought to my attention. Bits of old glass and ceramics, tarnished and corroded ammunition brass and lead, aboriginal pottery sherds, chips of flint, old nails and tacks, rusty cans, buttons, coins, and other odd items are frequently revealed to me, as one or more birds may be heard clattering around with curious things in their bills. These turkeys commonly carry strange objects in their bills for short distances. Any peculiar thing in our vicinity will eventually be examined and toyed with by everyone.

Bones seem to be particularly interesting to wild turkeys, and although they will eat an occasional chip of bone, they seem also to be intrigued by the unusual shapes and textures. I once saw one of the hens casually transporting the skull of a possum. Eventually, she lost interest and dropped it without looking back. Several others immediately began playing with it. In this way, we manage to survey much of what has had occasion to die in this area. We visit several sites with regularity where skeletons lie, and the birds never seem to tire of studying them. When approaching a particular skeleton for the first time, however, they can be extremely cautious.

Feathers are always objects of curiosity, and it is almost impossible for any of these wild turkeys to pass by one without picking it up at least once. All small feathers, when found or molted, are immediately eaten.

Old weathered, flat-sawn pine stumps, standing in the field or woods, are regarded with great concern and will be scrutinized. Naturally occurring stumps, although interesting, are not considered disturbing. Similarly, if a limb or branch has fallen in an area that we traverse regularly, it is often identified as something out of order and viewed with caution.

Day-Glo surveyor's tape is on first encounter regarded with caution and fear (turkey hunters take note). After daily exposure, eventually they disregard it.

Should I ever stop to examine something, whether plant, animal, or object of any kind, everyone immediately halts other activities and gathers around. Generally, they do not come barging in pecking at things but rather stand very close and quietly observe. After I examine the object, they will in turn continue the inquiry, which may involve pecking or tapping the object with their bills.

Occasionally, I spot insects or spiders that they have failed to see. If I point with my finger at a nearby object, they readily know to look for and find the object, rather than staring at my finger. Even dogs have some difficulty making that type of indirect association.

I have never kept better company or known more fulfilling companionship. Our communication, although somewhat abstract, is completely satisfying, and our interests are identical: plants, insects, reptiles, birds, mammals, the odd bone, interesting artifacts. We are driven by the same engine, and, in spite of our divergent morphology and intellectual approach, I find that in the most fundamental sense, our similarities are greater than our differences.

As we near Bert's Branch, the turkeys sound the alarm again. This time it's a large gray rat snake. Now I just watch and feel no need to intervene. They are very interested and spend time laboriously examining him but eventually join me in the hammock by the branch. I watch as a turkey captures, kills, and eats a spring peeper (*Hyla crucifer*). We are eating frogs now! I am impressed.

The creek is high and noisy. The turkeys are intrigued and waste no time wading out into the relatively swift water. Later, we work down the creek and out of the hammock. I hear alarm putting again. They have found another diamondback—medium sized—about three to four feet. The turkeys all gather around as though curious, but this time they are very disturbed. They maintain a safe two- to three-foot distance from the snake as he lies coiled on the leaves of the forest floor. He rattles lightly at first, then more deliberately. The turkeys become very nervous and agitated. I observe an odd behavior that I have not seen before. Some stand on one foot and stamp the other rapidly in the leaves, producing a staccato thumping sound. This lasts for only a second or two and is then repeated by another turkey. They leave the rattlesnake reluctantly, only after I move on; they gradually catch up.

Soon we move into the big, spreading live oak. I climb up, and they all fly up around me. Limbing behavior ensues for the next twenty minutes or so as we relax—then work our way slowly back home in the afternoon. We had a great day.

July 20, Saturday

No rain falls today, and temperatures are around 100. Everyone seems healthy, and we concentrate on grasshoppers, which are particularly abundant.

We've been encountering a coyote with some regularity now. It is a relatively slight individual with a track that is smaller than the average, so I can keep up with its comings and goings. I suspect it is either very young or perhaps a small female.

This coyote is interested in these wild turkeys and bungles onto us occasionally. Several times, hearing alarm putts as heads rise up, I have caught a glimpse of her nervously skulking by with head and tail down. She is conspicuously active in the heat and light of day and on occasion will enter the area of the cabin in broad daylight, although I have not observed her near the pen.

Today, with a chatter and a quick burst of flight, the turkeys take refuge in the surrounding young pines. The birds protest with loud putts and jeer down as I am left standing face to face with God's dog, who suddenly becomes very humble. She guards her retreat with a retracted tail and sheepish glances over her shoulder. The indignant turkeys soon drop back to the ground and resume foraging.

We encounter a cranky black racer, an individual I suspect we have encountered before. The turkeys are cautious but seem to enjoy investigating and annoying the snake. As the day becomes hotter, we move

more or less directly to Bert's Branch. The water has receded a little, and we spend hours exploring the creek and surrounding hammock.

We see no snakes in the hammock today, and I think it is because of the intense heat. A solitary and lethargic box turtle is our only surprise. He merely closes his door and refuses to interact with the turkeys. We putt and crane a little and then proceed through the hammock.

The forest floor is still moist from all the rain, and we move quietly along. Insects and birds sing and call in the canopy but seem subdued by the heat. The air is still and heavy, but there is a damp coolness near the water. Tumbling from shallow pools over limestone shelves into other sparkling pools, the water is clear with a slight amber cast from filtering through the organic debris of the swamps. The sun dances through the overhanging vegetation, producing an ever-changing kaleidoscope of light and shadow on the sandy bottom of the stream. Light is in turn reflected up and illuminates the undersides of the branches that overhang the sparkling water. The turkeys appear enchanted by this mysterious shimmering spectacle and spend much of their time quietly observing the phenomenon. It is good to see that they are completely at home here. They appear to be a perfectly integrated part of a much greater experience. I am envious.

A water thrush, furtive and sensual, nods along, flitting from one rocky pool to the next like a water spirit, occasionally flipping fallen leaves—probing—prospecting for life. Both leopard and bronze frogs are abundant, jumping before us, darting underwater and seeking refuge. There is a serenity about this branch today that is conveyed to the turkeys, and they respond by behaving in a manner that brings the word majestic to mind. Moving as slowly and as quietly as possible, I sit and try to become invisible. A wild turkey approaches and sits on my lap. I am honored. Perhaps she thinks I belong.

July 21, Sunday

Claudia's family comes today, so we will not have an opportunity to forage. I do, however, find considerable time to spend with the turkeys. They are accepting of the guests from a distance but find their odd color combinations disturbing and respond occasionally with loud, coarse yelping. Someone sneezes, and spontaneous gobbling by two or three jakes occurs. The gobbling, although of a high pitch, is very well articulated. I have heard wild jakes one year old do much worse.

The continuous rain and warm temperatures cause the snakes to be very active. Today, I removed another large diamondback rattlesnake as it passed within sight of the cabin. A male, judging by his relatively slender conformation, with an incomplete rattle of sixteen remaining segments, he is well over five feet in length.

Yesterday I captured a beautifully marked, thirty-inch cottonmouth moccasin near the steps of the cabin. She has already found a new home several miles up the river.

I am a little nervous about all this snake activity, but I find that the rotten log pile seems a lonely place now, and I miss the great rattlesnake's quiet presence there. I have been forced to draw the line for safety's sake, I suppose.

July 22, Monday

The weather is incredibly hot today. The turkeys are panting early, holding their wings out and down. I am worried about one of the hens, who seems a little peculiar today, tucking her head and sleeping constantly, so I add medication to the water and watch her closely. She seems weak and appears to have difficulty swallowing. I observe her in our activities throughout the day, and she gradually improves.

Today, I bring a small, high-resolution video camera that will fit comfortably in my pack. I have been reluctant to do this, but some of what I'm observing needs to be recorded on tape. As we move slowly along, I get shots of general behaviors like stripping seeds, foraging, and collecting deer berries. The heat is intense. We find some gopher tortoise burrows and spend time dusting. The battery of the camera gives out after about twenty minutes of footage. Surely now we will encounter something remarkable. We cut across the northern part of the field and hit the dim roadbed. Heading south toward home, I see fresh deer tracks and admire the turkeys' tracks as they are being created, noticing that they are indistinguishable from the mature resident wild turkey tracks. As we pass the rotten log pile on our left, I proceed with great care, as if the rattlesnake could still be near, feeling a part of her that remains in this place. I carefully complete the fifty or so feet past her realm with the turkeys following. Alarm putts go out behind me. I can't believe it. This must be a mistake—but I know the turkeys very rarely make mistakes in these matters. They are standing in a semicircle craning and putting between the old roadbed and the logs, where the grass is thick and green. Bewildered, I see that I have walked within three feet of another rattlesnake and, in spite of my best efforts to do otherwise, missed it entirely. This snake, although respectable, is not like the awesome matriarch that lived here before. Feeling a strange sense of gratification that there are still rattlesnakes here, I also worry that there are so many. The turkeys are obsessively curious and are beginning to concern me. I make the alarm purr, but they only continue with craning necks and loud putting. Suddenly, the snake makes a short, blind strike, breaks coil, and leaps for the cover of the logs. In that instant the turkeys explode into flight, making a sound that I am sure can be heard for a great distance. I am actually hit by a couple of turkeys as they speed through the air. We cautiously head for home, our vigilance renewed. A few blackberries remain and are well ripened. They are all eaten in seconds, and we press on. The turkeys readily follow me into the pen. The little hen who seemed weak this morning did well on our walk. I notice sores on the heads of some individuals—probably the first signs of fowl pox.

July 23, Tuesday

The heat index is 110 degrees today. I open another fifty pounds of turkey feed. The turkeys' intake of food grows exponentially, along with their size. They finished the last bag yesterday. It is too hot to move. Later we can walk if it clouds over. The little hen seems okay today, so I discontinue the medication in their water.

The insects love this weather, and gnats are particularly bad today. They remain constantly near my eyes and ears as they swarm by the hundreds around me. The turkeys are also annoyed and frequently rub their heads on their backs. I take the video camera today, and the battery runs short again but is adequate.

We make a loop up through the field and then enter the hammock surrounding Bert's Branch. The turkeys become very alarmed at one point while near the creek, but I never find out why.

We slowly work our way out of the branch and back home. It is nearly dark, so the turkeys drink water and immediately fly up on the roost. Addled by the gnats, I am glad to call it a day. I have never known these particular biting gnats to be a problem here. This is a very odd year—all things that can bite are abundant. My neck and elbows itch and burn.

Wild turkeys have enormous enthusiasm for life. From the moment they leave the egg, they are exuberant and aggressive. Birds in general display very little of the youthful enthusiasm seen in mammals, and young wild turkeys in particular seem disinclined toward anything resembling play—they are born with an intriguing level of maturity. Coupling this with a remarkable preexisting genetic understanding of the various aspects of their environment, they possess from birth a graceful integrity and presence that defy their age. So much detailed genetic information is being passed on through these birds that it seems they are born ancient. Wild turkeys, and birds in general, predate us by an enormous antiquity. Our oldest bipedal ancestor was preceded by the wild turkey by tens of millions of years.

Observing these birds from day to day, I find that there is still so much I do not understand about their activities and behaviors. Often

Comparative anterior view of tarsometatarsus (lower leg) from fossil (L) and contemporary (R) wild turkey gobbler (Meleagris gallopavo).

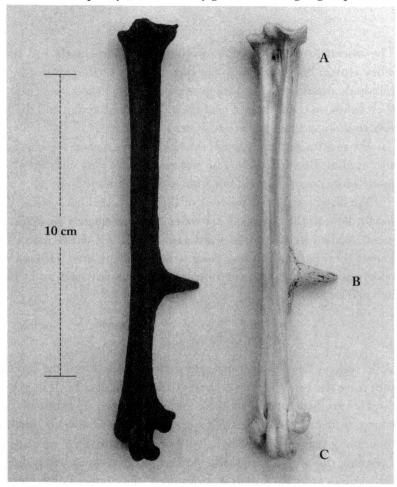

A. hypotarsus (damaged on fossil specimen)
B. spur core
C. digital articulations (trochlea)

The darker fossil specimen was recovered in Jefferson County, Florida, in association with other late Pleistocene species, including horse, bison, camel, giant sloth, mammoth, and mastodon.

I notice that wild turkey vocalizations within the flock are an emotional response or an audible reinforcement to a silent communication that has obviously already occurred. In addition to this communication, which is inaccessible to me, I perceive other distinct behaviors that defy explanation. Certainly they are capable of observing dangers and events that I fail to see or hear, but sometimes their reaction is more extreme than necessary to avoid the coyote, for example, which although a bother, is a threat easily dealt with. On occasion, it seems they react to something that is not actually present. It is a curious event and often leaves me spinning in a circle as I try to locate the source of their strange apprehension.

Generally, wild turkeys are quite composed in the face of danger; they are not prone to waste energy by overreacting to threatening stimuli. A genetic program that must be very detailed and taxonomically comprehensive allows these birds to know virtually from birth with near perfect accuracy what is edible, what is dangerous, who is friend, and who is foe. These behavioral mechanisms appear to come pre-installed in the wild turkey's brain and require only the appropriate sight or sound to trigger instant recognition and corresponding appropriate response. This is as it should be, for turkeys are born in a combat zone of sorts. Time is a luxury that a young wild turkey cannot afford.

I wonder on occasion when I think they are "overreacting" if perhaps I am observing what I have come to regard speculatively as vestigial or "fossil behavior." For example, take the Florida panther, not yet an extinct species, but extinct within the range of these birds and their immediate ancestors. No relative of these wild turkeys has had a panther encounter for perhaps forty or fifty years. A cat that is capable of springing thirty feet from a concealed location could have dictated the development of some unique compensatory behaviors.

Looking a little farther back, William Bartram, the naturalist who traversed North Florida in the late 1700s, mentioned the existence of large packs of black wolves. Although these wolves are generally believed to be an extinct subspecies or color phase of the now gravely endangered red wolf, we actually know nothing of their behavior or of their predatory relationship to the wild turkey.

The late Pleistocene, which is evolutionarily only yesterday to a twenty-million-year-old bird, was replete with formidable predators. Florida probably resembled East Africa during much of that period. The wild turkey shared this land with a wide variety of extinct cats, including a giant lion that was perhaps 50 percent larger than the contemporary African variety, several species of saber-toothed cats, as well as another species of lion that closely resembled contemporary African lions, and numerous species of smaller extinct cats, including jaguars. There were wild dogs and the great dire wolf, which was larger than the contemporary gray or timber wolf of the North.

Considering the detailed distinctions and behaviors retained in the wild turkey's brain relative to contemporary plants, insects, reptiles, mammals, and birds, it seems possible, therefore, that very specific knowledge could be retained regarding these predators of antiquity. The wild turkey may still anticipate species that no longer exist. Biology is slow to relinquish those attributes that have served survival well.

We human beings also have ancient genetic information stored in our contemporary brains that could be said to approximate the vestiges of fossil behavior. Human infants exhibit a fear of heights that could have its origin as far back as our arboreal ancestors. And how easily people are made to feel revulsion at the sight of snakes, spiders, or insects, though the automobile, infinitely more dangerous and deadly, cannot through association be made to make us cringe and shudder. The chill bumps that people experience at times of fear are the behavioral vestiges of a past when we had sufficient fur that, when raised, would afford us a more imposing silhouette. We all have a fossil past— a living genetic link to our most remote antiquity.

I find it impossible to consider the wild turkey without attempting to place them on a continuum of enormous antiquity. Tree-dwelling birds and waterfowl appear to be relatively indifferent to the large inhabitants with which they share the land. But the wild turkey's peculiar adaptation as principally a ground-dwelling bird, coupled with its unusually large size, makes it a significant and potentially accessible meal, which has probably exposed it to environmental pressures unknown to many other bird species.

July 24, Wednesday

We leave the pen early this A.M. in hopes of doing some serious foraging before the temperature becomes unbearable. The morning is hazy and overcast. Radiant heat, or direct exposure to the sun, tends to stress the turkeys more than ambient heat. Their dark bodies must absorb much of the sun's radiation.

I carry the video camera as we pass through the field and enter the hammock surrounding Bert's Branch. We spend much time here—me sitting and observing with the camera—the turkeys forage, explore, limb, wade, and generally enjoy the branch.

Two turkeys are toying with something in the water. They have been ambitiously scratching in the water, which they often do. I look closely. They have pulled up from the mud and sand covering the lime-stone bottom a perfect abo-riginal projectile point—an arrowhead. The whitish point shines on the dark, silty sand, glisten-ing under the current. Several turkeys are attracted to the object and in turn come by to examine it. We are all drawn to the artifact—it is something special. Their interest eventually wanes, and I lift the point from the water—the first human to touch this object in thousands of years.

The point is made of a pinkish white flint that looks local in origin. It is 1³/₄ inches long, 1³/₁₆ inches wide, and reasonably well made over-all, with excellent fine chipping on the sides out to the tip, which is very sharp. I recognize this point as originating in the "middle archaic" period, from a tradition known to southeastern archaeologists as Savan-nah River. Dating from four to six thousand years before the present, these points are characterized by a stemmed, rather square base, with a slightly concave bottom edge. Middle archaic people were seminomadic hunters and gatherers whose traditions covered large geographic areas with very gradual changes in tool assemblages. Archaic trash middens, when excavated, usually reveal a few stone tools with points not unlike this one and a wide variety of animal bones. Typically included are a preponderance of deer, along with bear, raccoon, other small mammals, fish, reptiles, and one of the most common bird bones found in these ancient middens—*Maleagris gallopavo,* the wild turkey.

We spend time in the field as well as the branch. The day is overcast but very hot. While examining the dead tortoise, some other bones are found nearby, as well as a handful of hawk feathers. Snakes have been scarce for the past two days—they don't seem to like this dry heat.

The turkeys make a bit of a stir over a box turtle hidden under a deer berry bush. Wild turkeys seem to naturally bear resentment toward anything that tries to conceal itself from them. A small snake or turtle that would be ignored in plain view will often create a chorus of protest as the turkeys identify and expose its whereabouts.

We arrive home before sunset, and I sit with the turkeys for a while. A palpable feeling of connectedness envelops us. We are very close. This has been a full and productive day for us.

It is interesting that each time we pass the rotten log pile, the turkeys look closely in the vicinity of the rattlesnake's previous location. They have a specific memory of that event.

July 25, Thursday

Soul-wetting, unrelenting rain. Something has happened to scare the turkeys, and several have abrasions on their bills from hitting the wire. Spooky lost four of her pretty new tail feathers. There are no tracks around the pen. Maybe a hawk or an owl?

July 27, Saturday

Another rainy day with storms all around. We find a couple of hours in midafternoon to forage between showers. I carry the video camera and a plastic bag to put it in if the rain comes, which it does but not in great quantity. A light shower falls while the sun shines. It is quite beautiful.

We forage up through the field and eventually pass by the rotten log pile. The turkeys, as usual, inspect the area carefully. I see nothing, but they immediately find another rattlesnake—probably the same one we saw a couple of days ago. About three feet in length and unusually dark, he is so difficult to see in the grass that I am intimidated. I spend considerable time taping the turkeys as they inspect the snake with craning necks and much vocalization.

Their interest in snakes has always bothered me, as I have feared that they could be killed or injured. Now, however, I let them do what they want and realize that this exaggerated interest in things that may or may not be dangerous probably serves their need for specific information. In an environment where so many hazards exist, ignorance has no survival value. In addition to extraordinary instinctive or genetic understanding, wild turkeys also have a remarkable ability to learn, never having to be shown anything a second time. These birds are highly motivated students, and class is always in session.

The gnats are very annoying again today. The turkeys constantly shake their heads and rub their faces on their backs. I have never before experienced a gnat problem here that persisted throughout the summer, and so I collected a few specimens, including some engorged individuals, for identification at the Cooperative Extension Service at the University of Florida in Gainesville. I was told that they belong to the order Diptera, which includes many biting and bloodsucking insects, not the least of which are the mosquitoes. The notorious black fly of the North Woods is a member of the same genus. This particular relatively large gnat has been tentatively identified as *Simulium meridional*. The folks at CES have conveniently assigned it the common name "turkey gnat" (probably in hopes that I will be somehow consoled), which I concur is as good as any. Unfortunately, this pest, they tell me, is immune to "chemical controls." I have found that if I apply an oily repellent thick enough, occasionally one will drown—otherwise, they are indifferent. It would be interesting to know how wild turkey populations in general are affected by this gnat, and if it constitutes a significant disease vector. These insects have been known to be carriers of avian malaria. It is apparent that the sores occurring on the heads of many individuals with fowl pox represent particular inoculation sites inflicted by this relentlessly tormenting gnat.

July 28, Sunday

The weather is threatening early in spite of a beautifully clear, full-moon night. I have coffee and visit with the turkeys as the sun rises over Bert's Branch hammock. The jake I refer to as Turkey Boy is keeping one of his eyes closed most of the time. I assume he has injured it somehow.

Afternoon is extremely hot and completely overcast—the turkeys pant and droop their wings. Rain falls briefly around three, and the temperature drops at last.

We forage up toward the forest, exploring the margin of the hammock between Bert's Branch and the east side of the old field. This is an interesting area environmentally as a particularly poor, sandy part of the old field gives way to the relative richness of the hammock and the creek. In his pioneering work *Game Management,* Aldo Leopold articulates many of the fundamental principles of wildlife management still in use today. In his discussion of "game range" and "interspersion," he describes the environmental phenomenon that he refers to as the "edge effect" simply as "simultaneous access to more than one environmental type," as at the edges of agricultural areas; the edges of roads, trails, or paths; fencerows; and the margin between one type of woodland and another. Frequently, a particular species' distribution is determined, within a given range, by the locations where multiple environmental zones intersect and overlap. This particular location on the edge of the old field is an area where almost every environmental type known to this region is represented "simultaneously."

A relatively dry and sandy or "xeric" ridge dotted with scrubby live oaks, a few stunted longleaf pines, and lichens for ground cover abruptly ends and falls away to a moderately moist and rich zone of mixed hardwoods that would be considered environmentally "mesic." Surrounding this area within a stone's throw on the north and on the southwest are two bay swamps that are environmentally very different. One understory is characterized by wild azalea and gallberry, the other to the north by abundant titi and viburnum. These areas also immediately intersect the more "riparian" zone of the limestone-bottom creek, which falls along the Sopchoppy River floodplain. Additionally, across the creek through the adjacent hammock lies an old agricultural field occasionally planted in corn.

As a result of so much ecological variety in one location, environmental types that in our area represent only marginally good wildlife habitat together create a rich and diverse biological community.

Today we find a late-blooming blueberry (*Vaccinium corymbosum*, I believe) loaded with berries. In spite of the presence of deer berry all around (*Vaccinium stamineum*), the turkeys recognize the former as an unusual treat and consume the vast majority of ripe ones. Young wild turkeys appear to be very selective and usually choose berries that are perfectly ripe. They never pull an unripe berry from a bush, and likewise they are hesitant to eat overripe berries from the ground. Oddly, after eating a few berries from one bush, they are likely to move on to another bush, leaving perfectly good fruit behind. They are not predisposed to overindulge. Occasionally, we encounter emerging or pupating grasshoppers. As we approach, a fountain of young grasshoppers will spew forth from a single location in the grass. Rather than harvesting the entire family, each poult will enthusiastically eat several, then move on and search for other grasshoppers, leaving many behind. I find this behavior intriguing, and, although I am sure there are sound biological reasons for it, I admire it from a purely personal perspective.

After entering the hammock and slowly foraging along the creek, we encounter a freshly dropped primary flight feather from an adult wild turkey. I watch as the turkeys examine the feather with a quiet concern that makes me wonder how they differentiate this particular one from the similar juvenile flight feathers that drop occasionally while on our walks. I distinctly perceive a recognition and a respectful caution in their inquiry. These are the kinds of behaviors that fascinate me so much. That they might recognize this feather as one of their kind, yet differentiate it from one of their own, is to me an incredible notion. I am constantly reminded that these birds have innate knowledge that facilitates the recognition of things previously unknown: the ability to distinguish the silhouette of a soaring hawk from that of a vulture at a thousand feet; recognizing a venomous snake as more dangerous than a nonpoisonous one; complete insect recognition regarding palatability and danger. All of these attributes are manifest almost from birth with no need of trial and error. The turkeys just already know. It is the specificity of this knowledge that is so remarkable.

We locate an area within the hammock where resident wild turkeys have scratched in the leaf mulch of the forest floor. Upon seeing the remains of this activity, these turkeys begin scratching in the leaf mulch themselves. I watch to see if something unusual turns up here, but the earlier activity appears to have been arbitrary and we lose interest after a few fruitless minutes.

Moving from the hammock back out into the old field, we make a sweep up through some old abandoned beehives toward the north. We pass an active gopher tortoise burrow, and the turkeys, of course, must always examine these carefully, checking for large, furry wolf spiders, which frequent the twilight area of the opening, and sampling the sandy overburden from within for grit and dusting potential. I examine a large rattlesnake skin shed a few feet away. It is not fresh, and the turkeys, surprisingly, acknowledge its presence but are otherwise uninterested. As we browse down the west side of the field, the turkeys begin putting cautiously but quietly and point out a beautifully marked box turtle, partially hidden among some bog buttons. We crane briefly and move on.

We return at sunset, and I remain with the turkeys until after dark. We roost together, and I feel guilty when I quietly slip away in the night.

July 29, Monday

It is obviously going to be another nasty day. Storms are all around, and the sky is completely overcast—the air is muggy.

A large pine limb has fallen beside the turkey pen. The turkeys are still upset when I arrive, and many of them have abrasions on their heads and bills from striking the wire. None appears seriously injured, but they are very nervous.

We leave the pen early, foraging through the field, and soon encounter a black racer that has attempted to cross an open, grassy area. Only about half the group stops to examine him; the others move on unimpressed. They are such veterans now with the rattlesnakes that other snakes are unexciting by comparison.

Continuing up through the old field grazing on grasshoppers, seeds, and the like, we hit the old roadbed, go directly to the northern end of the field, and see a deer running up ahead. We enter Bert's Branch at the northern end by way of an old overgrown road that once forded the branch. We cross over and spend considerable time exploring down the east side of the creek. This is all new territory for the turkeys, who are very alert and cautious. They seem pleased to be exploring new hammock land and make contented vocalizations as we move slowly through the woods. After briefly examining another empty gopher tortoise carapace, we find more ripe blueberries on this side of the creek. The undergrowth becomes very dense, so we move into the run of the creek, eventually finding a place to cross back over. This particular spot appears somehow pleasing and interesting to the birds, and they stop here by the water to rest. Standing quietly, they observe carefully and listen, their movements very slow and deliberate. We remain in this state for thirty minutes or so and then begin lazily moving down the west side of the branch. It is thick here with large specimens of wild azalea. The dark waxy leaves of dog hobble (*Leucothoe axillaris*) and highbush gallberry (*Ilex coriacea*) are abundant, making the hammock appear somber under the overcast sky. We finally reach the northern limit of one of our previous walks and begin to recognize familiar woods. The solemn atmosphere in the hammock serves to make the turkeys' progress down the creek very relaxed and slow. They seem more interested in exploration and observation than in hunting for food. Wild turkeys often seem to be profoundly motivated by wonder.

It is impossible to ignore the extraordinary state of awareness in these wild birds. As I watch them contemplate and scrutinize, it is difficult to describe much of their nature or various behaviors without resorting to the word "consciousness." They seem in some way to epitomize that word. Although linguists, neurobiologists, psychologists, and even vertebrate paleontologists all claim insight into the strange fabric of consciousness, they are noticeably careful to avoid a comprehensive definition of the subject. Consciousness is that mysterious realm in which matter becomes so sufficiently organized that it may begin to contemplate itself. All of our quantitative empirical understanding tends to fall apart as we begin to observe the source of our own perception. For a scientist, the door of perception can be the entrance to a house of cards. Consciousness is everything that science is not—abstract, subjective, and qualitative. It is probably the height of irony that reason should attempt to proceed from such a place. But consciousness does have an organic, biological origin, and so it is possible to understand some of the mechanics involved.

Robert Ornstein's *The Evolution of Consciousness* and Israel Rosenfield's *The Strange, Familiar and Forgotten—An Anatomy of Consciousness* offer insight into the evolutionary mechanics of consciousness. Derek Bickerton's study *Language and Species* is very helpful in clarifying how representational systems and language enter into the conscious experience. Most researchers are in agreement that certain neurological functions must be in place before consciousness can be said to occur. These functions include such basic attributes as awareness of one's body; awareness of one's surroundings or space; memory; and the integrated continuity that these elements afford an organism through time. It is interesting to note that none of these attributes is particularly human, nor do they necessarily involve processes that one would associate with so-called higher brain function. After all, even a rechargeable battery has a memory, and as for the other attributes, it can be argued that they generally are present, to some degree, in the most primitive organism.

Rosenfield admits that animals are probably conscious but differ from humans in that "they do not contemplate their consciousness." This seems reasonable to me, although it may be presumptuous to suppose that they are absolutely incapable of that type of self-awareness.

Undoubtedly, it is the complex nature of language that would define a particular consciousness as being discretely human. Rosenfield considers that "the abstract nature of language is the ultimate form of consciousness." This strikes me as anthropocentric, and I would suggest that language merely defines the ultimate form of human consciousness. If wild turkeys had humanlike consciousness, they would all be dead in a day. Within the evolutionary scheme of things, our peculiar human consciousness has emerged only recently, relative to our more "unconscious" neurobiological faculties. As such, human consciousness could even be suspected of lacking great biological sophistication compared to the more ancient systems of the brain. "Antiquity" does not necessarily imply that which is primitive. To the contrary, biological systems tend to become more sophisticated and well tuned over time.

It is easy to demonstrate how the more unconscious systems of the brain operate. Remember learning to use a stick shift in an automobile, or learning an athletic sport. How awkward are our conscious attempts, until at last our unconscious minds can take control, and eventually we experience ourselves performing smoothly and without effort. It is very common for a musician to have the experience of being an impartial observer as his body and unconscious mind create beautiful music. Even that mysterious human moral regulator, our conscience, seems to impose itself upon us as a virtuous tap on the shoulder of our disconnected conscious awareness. Our plodding, methodical human consciousness enables us to actually control and train a more functionally elegant aspect of our being. These qualities that humanity seemingly admires and identifies as our "higher" nature could well have their origin in a being that lacked a consciousness defined by language.

Derek Bickerton reminds us that as humans we have "no privileged access to reality" and warns that "the opening of the gates of consciousness is in fact a progressive distancing of the creature from the actual world of external objects and events." He describes this phenomenon as "the paradox of consciousness—that the more consciousness one has, the more layers of processing divide one from the world."

Many researchers seem to be in agreement that our consciousness is identified by a language-based representational system that is unique among all of life; it enables us to organize and synthesize vast amounts of information through symbolization, to make intellectual abstractions, and to create culture. But I would suggest that human consciousness could be viewed as more of a nervous bureaucracy than a state of sentient awareness.

By the definitions above, science appears to be describing an existential consciousness, an awareness of self that can ultimately alienate one entirely from the rest of the universe, creating a sense of isolation, vulnerability, and mortality—the existential human dilemma. This could be uniquely human, a result of a highly developed language-based brain function. Human existential alienation seems to be in opposition to a fully conscious and nonverbal experience that the esoteric religions have identified and utilized for thousands of years to manifest psychological and spiritual union of the individual with the universe. This experience may precede, evolutionarily, the abstract nature of the human mind. Perhaps in our whirlwind evolutionary journey we have misplaced a vital aspect of our being that we would do well to recover.

The turkeys are reluctant to leave the branch and are slow to follow me out of the hammock. Thunder threatens from the southwest, so we move in the general direction of home. The openness of the field revives their interest in foraging, and they again move rapidly, collecting deer berries and capturing grasshoppers.

When we reach the lower end of the field, the storm seems no closer so we continue browsing. Finding an attractive spot beneath a young spreading pine where the gnats are not troublesome, we sit together, comfortably overlooking the open field. A family of crows makes the old field cheerful with its activity and noise. A titmouse calls from the adjacent hammock fifty yards away. A speaker of fluent titmouse, I answer. A short conversation ensues. Looking around, I see that all my companions seem to have little question marks over their heads, so I suspend dialogue with the titmouse.

We return to the pen in late afternoon feeling very good. All the tension of the morning has been relieved.

Seeing a primary flight feather freshly dropped from a red-shouldered hawk today, I noticed the wider transverse white bands but also that it superficially resembles that of a wild turkey. Two poults examined it briefly, and one pecked at it and walked on—a totally different response than the keen interest the turkeys displayed yesterday over the adult wild turkey primary.

July 31, Wednesday

After an all-day storm on Tuesday and a restless night fraught with thunder and lightning, I awake to a cloudy but very pleasant morning. The wind is from the northeast and has a coolness that we have not felt in months. When I arrive at the pen with my coffee, the turkeys are already down and excited by the weather. There is a lot of not-so-serious sparring going on. The altercations appear to be random and not sex related, with hens often confronting jakes.

After I put a battery in my video camera, we go steadily to the northern end of the old field. The turkeys forage casually, and I can tell they are relieved to be out. We quickly find a quiet spot in some thick longleaf pines to relax for an hour or so. It is good to be out again—it is as though we need to reconstitute—and soon we all remember who we are and what we are doing here together.

Very gradually, we begin to move along up through the field. A cool breeze blows through the damp grass, occasionally lifting the turkeys' feathers. Wild turkeys are very stoic but do seem to have moods. Today I can feel that everyone is glad to be here. Grasshoppers are wet and fly poorly so are easily captured. We visit the late-blooming blackberry patch near the national forest. There are few things in life that a wild turkey loves more than a plump ripe blackberry. I am forced to participate in this effort myself, and in a matter of minutes we slip away through the grass like fat, guilty bandits, the evidence showing on our purple mouths.

Making a wide loop up into the extreme northwest corner of the old field, we visit some areas previously avoided because of thick palmettos and tall stiff grass. Snaking our way through in single file, we manage to find our way back to more open ground.

Hearing light, cautionary putting behind, I go back and investigate. Several turkeys are craning at a low, spreading bough from a young pine that is grown up in a thick bed of broom grass. I look closely and see nothing. I can tell by their voices and behavior that it is not a rattlesnake. I very slowly lift up the bough from the end as more turkeys gather around. Cautiously, I expose a young cottontail rabbit—maybe four or five inches from nose to tail—and it remains absolutely motionless. As the rabbit is exposed to the view of the turkeys, all look closely but appear in no sense alarmed. They show only a keen but quiet interest in the odd, furry little thing with the big, wet, intensely black eyes. I gently lower the pine bough back over the little rabbit, and we quietly move on, our curiosity with rabbits at last having been somewhat satisfied.

With a steady breeze and the sun shining infrequently, we head across the field toward Bert's Branch after a short limbing session in a spreading longleaf pine. The branch is lively from a night of heavy rain, and the cool damp air is moving inside the hammock. We go to the water's edge and are refreshed. The turkeys indicate that they are pleased with this location and would like to remain here, so I find a pretty vantage point overlooking the creek and get comfortable. Stretching, preening, and faintly purring, they appear to be in heaven, and we spend a couple of very pleasant hours "nooning." Eventually, I find myself sitting in a small area of sunlight with a pile of wild turkeys sleeping and resting all around. This seems to be the mode of the day, and by listening to every subtle sound, we engage in activities like bird-song identification and familiarization. Wild turkeys, it seems, are very attentive to other birds in general and appear to want to become familiar with all of them, including their songs and various noises. Today Bert's Branch is a stream of consciousness. A red-shouldered hawk shares the hammock, and the turkeys become displeased over this on several occasions, but generally he keeps his distance. Even when relaxed, these young wild turkeys remain vigilant.

Because of our closeness and familiarity, it is easy for me to lose sight of just how wary and "wild" these birds really are. Frequently, I am jolted into remembering this by an explosion of flight that occurs around me—many times in response to dangers I have completely failed to perceive. As humans, we arrogantly identify wildness in animals merely as the fear they exhibit in response to us. In reality, except for a short period of time during hunting season, we are relatively insignificant to wild turkeys and one of the least of their worries in the daily scheme of things.

Slowly we move down and eventually out of the hammock by way of the rotten log pile. Arriving at the logs with the turkeys lazily following, I have time to check the surrounding grass carefully for inhabitants and see nothing. I want to record the turkeys' cautionary behavior as they near the logs and so begin taping. As predicted, they do become very quiet and watchful as they approach. They work their way down the length of the logs, and as they arrive at my end, they begin staccato alarm putting at a rattlesnake coiled in the grass directly in front of my feet. Once again I am bewildered. I stop taping and take a look. This is a heavy-bodied snake about four feet in length, larger and more pale than the one we saw a couple of days ago. The turkeys all take a good look, and then we move on. I think their curiosity with rattlesnakes is beginning to be satisfied.

The temperature is very hot in spite of a continuous breeze. The turkeys seem to get tired by midafternoon, so we spend an hour or so in the big spreading live oak. They are reluctant to leave its sanctuary but eventually follow me back into the hammock.

Other encounters this afternoon include a large coach whip that is so shocked by so many wild turkey faces that he forgets to dash away. Consequently, we have the opportunity to study him closely. Later, after passing a lazy box turtle that the turkeys choose to generally ignore, we find a pygmy rattlesnake, and they once again behave as though they are unimpressed. The turkeys' behavior regarding reptiles is definitely changing.

We return to the pen before dark, having had a very full day. While I stand outside and videotape, they all enter the pen without any prompting from me—amazing.

August 1, Thursday

It is another beautiful, refreshing morning. I have my coffee with the turkeys, and then we begin our walk. After browsing the field for an hour or so, we head into Bert's Branch by way of the overgrown road that fords the stream. We cross over and head down the creek following the same general route we used several days earlier. Crossing back over Bert's Branch and very slowly working our way downstream, we encounter another pygmy rattlesnake coiled in the leaves near the branch. I see this one first and observe as several of the turkeys acknowledge his presence. None are terribly interested, and so we cross back over the branch again and continue down the east side, experiencing some new areas. The hammock is beautiful on this side, with some areas that are clean and open. I see a young spruce pine (*Pinus glabra*). These hammocks are full of old spruce pine stumps from trees that were all logged out many years ago.

We stop frequently at the attractive, accommodating places and relax. The turkeys find an abundance of food. Berries, butterfly larvae, smilax tips, various other insects, spiders, frogs, and seeds are eaten by the turkeys as I watch.

The afternoon and a certain lethargy overtake us. We eventually find ourselves sitting in the leaves, me against a comfortable hickory tree with legs outstretched and the turkeys around me, close, like small boats docked against a larger ship. They doze and preen while I tinker with my notes, the branch babbling just below us. With the soothing monotony of some mystical invocation, several red-eyed vireos transpose their own stream of rambling verse into the elusive rhythm of the flowing water. The whirring drone of cicadas combines into a soft mantric pulse. We are saturated by the moment, and I seem to become fundamentally interwoven with hickory, leaf mulch, and wild turkey. My boundaries become vague, my extremities obscure. I am part wood, part mulch, and part feathers.

All heads go up with a quick chatter of caution audible only to us. A steady rustle of leaves from up the creek—a pacing gray fox, obviously on a mission, hops across a downed log and trots along the opposite side of the

branch. As he comes near, several turkeys jump to their feet. The fox stops thirty yards away and stares intently with small penetrating black eyes. Motionless at first, his head then bobs several times as he tests the air. The turkeys are riveted and tense but do not appear fearful. Some part of me silently reaches out to this strange little fox like a lost friend. Once, a newborn fox from these very woods found her way into my life, and for a year or two our lives were intertwined. I remember her clean, warm, woodland scent—like freshly split oak in dry winter air—the cool moist touch of her nose on my face as I tried to sleep, and the familiar gentle tug on my hand of her needle-sharp teeth. We ranged for miles up and down the shallow streams. She was a ghostly specter who would suddenly appear and then dissolve away again—a study in the resolution of light and shadow, sound and silence, the crepuscular reconciliation of night and day. There is no creature more intense, more deliberate, or more uncompromising than the fox. Although there was no element of my being that could ever keep pace, she would graciously stay in secret, almost mystical orbit around me as I walked through her hidden world.

This fox suddenly lowers his head to the ground and takes a quick halting step in our direction. His head bobs again as he examines us. Suddenly, with a glance down the creek, he resumes his systematic gait—bushy tail held straight behind—his mission renewed.

Energized by our encounter with the gray fox, we cross the creek and work our way out of the hammock onto the edge of the old field. As we wander home late in the afternoon, I admire the turkeys and notice that they are in excellent condition. They are getting large and at a short distance are not particularly distinguishable from adult wild turkeys. Their legs are long and powerful. The feet are dark, and the jakes' tracks cannot be distinguished from those of the adult resident wild turkeys with which we share the area. The juvenile feathers are mostly replaced now, with third-molt feathers closing the centerline of the breast. The greater secondary coverts of the wing are more or less completely emerged. The bone and cartilage over the eyes have developed, giving the turkeys the fierce predatory look of mature birds. Tails are long and beautiful. I notice that the tails of the hens generally tend to stay better preserved. Graceful Samara, in particular, always keeps her plumage in perfect condition. When sitting in the woods now, I look around and see a beautiful flock of wild turkeys doing exactly what they should be doing.

August 3, Saturday

We begin our walk up through the field this morning, and it is already hot and muggy. The turkeys are ready to be out, and so am I. For whatever reason, the gnats are not bad today, but I am wearing a hot, long-sleeve, jersey T-shirt for the first time this summer. My elbows have become very sensitive from all the insect bites and at times are quite painful. I had better give them a break. I have also begun wearing my boots in an effort to reduce my chances of being snakebitten. We encounter venomous snakes almost every day, and the boots will at least protect me from the smaller ones. My snake awareness is at an all-time high as I expect to see them everywhere.

Soon after we begin our foray, the turkeys raise a fuss, and it is an attractive red rat snake, about three and a half feet long and rather dark. We have not encountered red rat snakes together before now, although I have seen them occasionally in the area over the years. The snake is out in the open on pine straw, under some large trees. He obviously feels vulnerable and is annoyed by all the attention from the birds. Assuming a threatening coil, and spreading his head as wide as possible, the angry snake makes an impressive show. The turkeys sense his displeasure and slowly move away. I make some cautionary turkey noise, and they seem to be in agreement.

We browse in the field, with emphasis on blackberries, which still occur in one area, and various green things, which seem particularly attractive to the turkeys today. It is hot, and we head for the shelter of the hammock and Bert's Branch. Passing two box turtles within several feet of each other, the turkeys make warning putts that are barely audible. The turtles are eyed with suspicion but otherwise ignored. We notice that deer berries, although still abundant, are beginning to wane. It will be a great loss when they are all gone.

The turkeys quickly move ahead of me in anticipation of the creek and line up along the water's edge. Immediately, their mood seems to change, and I get the sense that they would like to stay here for a while. I relax against the base of a large gnarly sparkleberry, and the turkeys begin enjoying the branch. They continue to be charmed by this place. Invariably spending much time just quietly looking around, they stretch frequently, standing on one foot and gracefully extending the opposing leg and wing. They also occasionally fluff up their feathers and shake off, which among birds in general often denotes a release of tension. The volume and frequency of contented purring is likewise conspicuous. This relaxed mood is highly contagious, and I feel my own awareness move out from my immediate vicinity and into the surrounding hammock. I can never tell in retrospect how much time we have spent in these pursuits. We are spellbound. It could be the crane flies, doing their strange pulsating dance in the filtered sunlight. Perhaps it's the whirligig beetles spinning circles in the shimmering current of the branch; or the green metallic damselfly's flashing flight, as she periodically and rhythmically flickers over the water to retrieve a gnat and predictably returns to the same perch. An enchantment suspends us in this place.

Suddenly a clap of thunder breaks very close, and I realize that a storm has moved in from the southwest. The turkeys are slow to follow me out of the hammock as rain begins to fall. I remembered to bring a plastic bag for my video camera. Water is fatal to video cameras, and lightning is fatal to me, so I am anxious to get to the shelter of home as soon as possible. I see a medium-sized rattlesnake coiled near the rotten log pile as I pass, but I don't slow down. Hoping that the turkeys will not get involved with the snake, I am relieved as they pass far enough away not to notice.

We arrive home in a downpour. The turkeys fly up on the roost under the dry roof, and I go inside the cabin. I hear them calling for me as I reach the door.

August 4, Sunday

I spend a rainy morning doing chores around the place and find time occasionally to sit with the turkeys.

Thunderstorms continue into the afternoon. Claudia and I are outside covering up the garden tractor when lightning strikes a tree very near the pen. I see the turkeys respond with some jumps, but no real explosive panic occurs. As we sit on the porch in the rain, we can smell smoke from the strike.

Late in the afternoon the turkeys and I go for a walk in a light rain. It is cool, and the land is lush. Raiding the grasses in skirmish-line fashion we find grasshoppers, spiders, and other insects to be abundant. Tree frogs are also frequently captured and eaten. I am very fond of frogs and go to considerable trouble to encourage their presence and

their welfare around here. But I must admit that I am delighted to see these wild turkeys aggressively taking them. There is something very correct about the process.

Our days are graced with an abundance of butterflies. Every different environment, depending on climate and physiography—latitude, elevation, soil type, moisture, and flora—has its own species of butterflies in varying proportions that will identify a given location with a particular signature. Although adult butterflies and moths do not seem to constitute a significant food source for wild turkeys, their larval forms are eaten in great quantity. On more than one occasion I have seen a turkey incited irresistibly to perform its happy dance in response to the inspirational company of a nearby butterfly.

We spend a couple of productive hours browsing and then head home.

August 5, Monday

The storms have passed, and the morning is once again hot and muggy. We spend the early part of the day foraging in the field—gnats are a bother. We pass a black racer that obviously is about to shed his skin, and the turkeys putt mildly at this shy serpent with the opaque milky goggles.

As soon as the turkeys have fed well in the field, we go into the hammock to escape the intense heat. We spend time foraging the hammock and eventually find an opportunity to relax in a relatively open area on the east side of the branch. Some of us sit and watch as others mill around feeding and exploring.

Birds of different species will, on occasion, band together in a large multispecies loose flock. This behavior may be observed daily in any woodland. Frequently, flocks of titmice, chickadees, and downy woodpeckers may be seen foraging through the woods together. And often many other species will join in.

Today, the largest mixed flock I have ever observed was organized and operating in Bert's Branch. I don't know the mechanisms involved that produce this behavior, but I do observe that, in general, birds are attracted to the activity of other birds. Many times the species involved do not share similar feeding habits, so obviously it is not merely feeding behavior that is at work in these cases. It is not uncommon for birds that eat only insects to be keeping company with species that eat primarily seeds. Typically, a mixed flock might consist of three or four species, with a total of fifteen or twenty individuals participating. The flock may slowly move along through an area, staying together for only a few minutes or as long as an hour or two. Then it disperses into its constituent subflocks or individuals. These congregations are usually quite loud, making mixed flocks easy to locate.

Within today's flock I observed titmice, chickadees, cardinals, blue jays, Carolina wrens, great crested flycatchers, red-eyed vireos, white-eyed vireos, downy woodpeckers, red-bellied woodpeckers, pileated woodpeckers, gnat catchers, towhees, catbirds, phoebes, and several species of warblers, including parula, yellow, hooded, and prothonotary. There were others that I could not positively identify, and all of these birds were in an area of about one acre. It was absolutely riotous. Whether it was coincidence or the turkeys contributed to all of this avian activity, whether the flock assembled around us or moved in, I

am not sure. In any case, the turkeys were beside themselves with all the noise and confusion.

As the chorus grew and intensified, the turkeys gave up all their activities and began intently observing the phenomenon with cocked heads. After an initial period of curiosity and apparent shyness, they soon began responding with curious clucks, putts, and some light yelping. This went on for probably thirty minutes. Birds were everywhere, flying in every direction and alighting all around us. I tried to remain as inconspicuous as possible. A jay amazed us all with an exciting acrobatic flight in pursuit of a terrified cicada, passing several times within a few feet of us. The tapping of woodpeckers could be heard constantly, and warblers were flitting everywhere after small insects.

After what seemed to be a very long time, the mixed flock moved off to the southwest, down the hammock, and things returned to normal. The turkeys then once again became relaxed and quiet.

We browse the field again in the afternoon. Deer berries are definitely becoming scarce.

Catching a black racer in the open under a young live oak, the turkeys gather around to observe but are not upset by the snake. The snake, however, becomes very angry and makes two lashing strikes at one of the turkeys, advancing toward the turkey after each strike. The turkey has no difficulty avoiding the aggressive snake and merely jumps back without becoming frightened. The snake then breaks his coil and makes a rapid semiprotected retreat. Most of the turkeys lose interest at this point, but a couple actually pursue the snake for a short distance.

I spend Monday night doing business and running errands, including buying another fifty pounds of turkey feed. I also buy some lightweight mesh camouflage clothes to wear in the woods with the turkeys. We are encountering other wild turkeys regularly, and I do not want to hinder possible interaction.

August 7, Wednesday

Since the temperature is supposed to be very high today, we start our walk before the sun rises. The turkeys are enthusiastic, so we spend much time foraging the old field. Grasshoppers are a big item today. I watch a turkey catch and eat a large buzzing cicada. These birds are very fond of them but seldom have an opportunity to indulge.

As the sun makes the field more uncomfortable, we work our way into the hammock and Bert's Branch. From midmorning on we leisurely go from one secluded location to another in the hammock. The turkeys browse and rest. We encounter two black racers, one gray rat snake, and two box turtles as we work our way north. We cross over the branch and start up the east side toward the overgrown ford. The turkeys are behind me, foraging slowly and contentedly. Consequently, I find myself moving ahead and waiting for them to catch up. As I

move across the branch, I wait thirty or forty feet away from the water. Finally, they begin arriving around me, and we again continue on our way. Suddenly, that particular kind of putting occurs ten feet behind me and slightly to my left. I turn and look but see nothing. More turkeys arrive and begin putting, and finally I see a fat rattlesnake coiled in some Virginia creeper near the base of a sweet bay. I have walked past another one. We have seen snakes all morning, and I have been trying to be conscious, but they are just maddeningly difficult to see. I record their response to the snake on video and quickly move on, making first the alarm purr and then the assembly yelp. I hear their putting in the thicket behind me as they continue to examine the snake. Finally, they all join me in a clearing under a canopy of live oak trees. We sit down, and some of them help me eat my apple as others browse some blueberries. Apples, I find, are the only food that I can carry that does not create too much of a distraction. Further, I can eat while walking, which is helpful.

While sitting at the base of a water oak overlooking the creek this morning, I took my old slate turkey caller out of my pack and began some soft *pit pit*. I call adequately with my mouth, and these birds are accustomed to it. But my voice does not carry, so in order to attract distant turkeys I used the yelper. This was new for these young turkeys, and they were extremely attentive. I then began some stronger, plain yelping. All heads were up, and everyone was motionless. As I occasionally yelped, I noticed the turkeys were not observing me but intensely studying the surrounding woods. One of the jakes was standing two or three feet directly in front of me, and suddenly I realized, as I softly continued yelping, that the sides of his face were turning a bright, rosy red. The other jakes were showing a similar change in color. The caruncles on their necks appeared to be unaffected, however. I stopped yelping, and the turkeys continued their vigil for some time before resuming normal behavior. The pale pink color returned to the sides of the jakes' heads after only a couple of minutes. I gathered from this that these turkeys were assuming I was communicating with other wild turkeys.

In almost three months spent with these wild turkeys I have observed very little aggressive behavior while on our daily outings. Occasionally, two turkeys will indulge in some ritualized, aggressive behavior, but usually it is very abbreviated and, with one exception, has not resulted in actual fighting. Fighting occurs between hens, between jakes, and between jakes and hens interchangeably. Submissive behavior occurs in similar combinations, with larger jakes frequently acting submissive toward a smaller female.

Strutting is very common in the pen but without exception does not occur when we are out. In the pen, hens are prone to strut occasionally but fail to indulge in the activity for an extended period of time. Hens typically will approach another turkey, swell quickly into the strutting posture, release a puff of air, and immediately resume other activities. On occasion, jakes will indulge in strutting behavior for several minutes. Hens will sometimes respond by assuming a submissive posture directly in front of the strutting male. This may result in awkward attempts by the male to mount the hen. Strutting is generally ignored by the other males.

I brushed my elbow on a poisonous saddleback caterpillar today. My poor elbows are in a constant histemic frenzy.

August 8, Thursday

We begin very early again, while the dew is heavy on the grasses. Feet and tails become wet after only a few minutes. It is a small price to pay to avoid the heat of the day.

Nearing the rotten log pile, we expect to see a rattlesnake sunning in the cool morning air, and we pass very carefully. Twenty feet past the logs pandemonium breaks out. We are all jumping around in the grass like popping corn as a terrified six-foot coach whip, unable to decide which route to take, frantically dashes among sixteen pairs of dancing legs. We have inadvertently surrounded a rotted-out stump that must be his home. He finally makes a dive into the dark cavity left by the dead tree and disappears. The disgruntled turkeys all gather

around the stump and peer briefly into the damp hole. None of us were looking for excitement this early in the day.

Regaining our composure, we browse on deer berries and grasshoppers along the margin of the hammock. The early morning air becomes muggy, so we head directly into the hammock and spend a quiet morning foraging along Bert's Branch. Smilax tips are very popular today. The turkeys seem to be spending more time scratching the forest floor, and occasionally I see them recovering and eating large butterfly or moth pupae, which live in the leaf mulch. Grass seeds are becoming abundant in the hammock, and the turkeys never seem to tire of stripping them off their stems. Lowbush gallberries (*Ilex glabra*) are common and are, without great enthusiasm, eaten (unlike deer berries) green or ripe. Fox grapes (*Vitis vulpina*) are showing up regularly and are very popular. The birds catch insects so quickly and aggressively now that I find it difficult to identify all that they are eating. The more significant things I observe them eating in the hammock include: earthworms; grasshoppers; crickets; katydids; cicadas; centipedes; all manner of spiders—the larger, the better—caterpillars and various other moth and butterfly larvae (although some, generally the furrier ones, are ignored); lizards, including green anoles and ground skinks; amphibians such as bronze frogs, spring peepers, pinewoods tree frogs, squirrel tree frogs, and green tree frogs; many types of beetles, excepting scarabs; and occasionally smaller butterflies and moths such as skippers and hairstreaks. Larger butterflies are generally ignored, although careless sulphurs are taken regularly. The large golden orb spiders (*Nephila clavipes*), often called banana spiders in this area, are abundant in these hammocks and are eaten in great quantity. The similar but more brilliantly marked argiope is also harvested in significant numbers. Both the silver and the larger black and yellow species are represented in this area.

August 9, Friday

In anticipation of another day approaching 100 degrees, we start out soon after daylight. Browsing in the field is very productive, although deer berries are becoming hard to find. Grasshoppers are still abundant, and cicadas are becoming either more common or easier to catch. Gnats are still very bad and, when coupled with the heat, drive us into the sanctuary of the hammock. We arrive at the creek while the air is still damp and cool from the long summer night. Mosquitoes, which have pestered us on earlier visits, are not a bother, and the gnats that follow us into the hammock quickly dissipate. Our mood changes, and in a few minutes we are calm and relaxed. While the turkeys enjoy wading in the creek, I watch a hen slowly stalking a leopard frog. Her technique is very catlike, although her final strike is distinctly reptilian. She is unsuccessful, as the wary frog makes a long leap into the water. Everyone is particularly nervous today about aerial predators, and I assume a hawk or owl was attracted to the pen at daylight. Such visitations seem to occur every few days.

Gradually foraging our way out of the hammock, we find a recently shed secondary flight feather from an adult wild turkey. A few minutes later the turkeys locate a primary feather. Having kept the adult wild turkey feathers that we occasionally find on our outings, I am now accumulating a sizable collection.

It is miserably hot.

Back in the pen, I spend an hour or two sitting with the turkeys and working on my field notes. It has rained this afternoon, and in a short time my clothes are dirty from wild turkey feet, as they all feel compelled to stand around on me.

At dark, as I stand among the shoulder-high roosting limbs, the turkeys all snuggle up close around me. They are much too big now to sit on my head or shoulders, but they do not realize this and still try. I receive a fairly bad scratch on my face from a hen who alights, slips off my head, and attempts to climb back up. The turkeys are approaching their juvenile or young adult size now and are quite heavy. Gradually, a peace settles over us, and all grow quiet. I eventually sneak off in the dark without a sound, curiously disappointed that I cannot stay the night.

Although it has been months since my first days with these turkeys, I am still fascinated by how complete our communication is. Even though our vocabulary is limited, I normally feel as though I understand perfectly what is being communicated. Sometimes I don't know exactly how this happens, but it definitely does. We are quite clear with each other. I try to let them determine as much as possible where we go and how we get there. However, when I want to make a change, there is never any dispute. With the exception of my incorrect vocalizations now and then, we have never had any significant miscommunication. I cannot distinguish all the subtle differences in their vocalizations, but somehow the subtle meaning is conveyed to me. Soon they will mature and become more independent, but I want to maintain this close communication for as long as possible.

August 10, Saturday

Now, as we leave the pen, the birds will frequently fly out to the edge of the field in anticipation of the day's adventure. Sometimes, after being distracted by interesting things just outside the pen, they all fly to join me as they realize I have begun without them. Early this morning several of the turkeys burst into flight in a wide quarter-mile circle around the lower end of the field, pitching in around the rest of us like large, feathered boomerangs.

Often now, with any small provocation, these birds will take flight. Young wild turkeys are much more inclined toward flight than are mature individuals—partially because of the exuberance of their youth but also because of their relatively light body weight. It is obvious that first-basic plumage is designed to serve a young but fully grown wild turkey. Consequently, these youthful birds are already wearing a plumage ultimately intended for a more mature bird. With extremely long tails and big broad wings, they have a high ratio of flight feathers to body weight, which makes flight relatively easy to attain.

Older wild turkeys, and in particular large adult gobblers, are more reluctant to take to the air. They prefer to elude trouble on foot, saving flight for trips to and from the roost and for real emergencies. It's not that they do not fly well, they are just conservative flyers.

Among young wild turkeys, however, it seems that flight is frequently a matter of pure inspiration. Each time they slip their earthly bonds and leave me behind, I experience a strange disappointment. I consider my flightless condition to be inconvenient and an overall handicap in this study. In my dreams I am unrestrained and, on occasion, find myself accompanying them quite naturally in that way. Surely, in some forgotten recess of our being there is a fundamental expectation of flight.

The morning is damp and cool, and these wild turkeys are excited about the prospects of a new day—of a new life. The gnats, although present, are not a great distraction. Proceeding up through the field, the turkeys establish a fast pace, dashing from one grasshopper to the next. We browse the northern part of the field and strip the remaining few blackberries from our late-blooming patch. Deer berries are drying up on the ground as the turkeys pluck one or two stragglers out of the bushes.

As I lead the way from under the cover of a young spreading live oak, I narrowly miss stepping on a pygmy rattlesnake. The turkeys are directly behind me. I observed a hen almost step unknowingly on a pygmy a few days ago, so I nervously give an alarm purr and jump to one side. In a panic, everyone runs for the cover of the live oak. I am sure they will think I have overreacted. Venturing back out, they see the snake and give him sufficient berth with only a few cautionary putts. A pygmy rattlesnake is no longer big news to these wild turkeys. I am embarrassed.

Heavy rains are predicted for most of the day. By late morning we see thunderheads rising and hear thunder in the southwest. Without ever entering the hammock, we forage down the east side of the field, carefully passing the rotten log pile. I see a freshly shed rattlesnake skin in the grass directly in front of the butt ends of the logs. After checking the surrounding grass over and over again, I carefully pick up the skin, which is still moist and supple—the diamond pattern is very clear. It is not broken or torn, so I decide to take this one home, and as I hold the skin, the strong pungent smell of rattlesnake musk is imparted to my hands. We have missed the actual event by a very short time.

On our way home, the turkeys putt cautiously at a low pine bough growing along the ground in the grass. I see nothing but slowly lift up the bough, exposing a black racer. The turkeys sound somewhat disturbed, possibly by the fact that he was attempting to be clever and hide from them—a fruitless effort. I lower the bough, and we return to the pen as storms move in.

August 11, Sunday

We begin early once again. Rain is promised. After raiding the old field for insects, we head for the hammock to escape the gnats and the rising sun. Many pleasant hours pass in the hammock, but as rain begins to threaten, we slowly move toward home.

While emerging from the hammock, the turkeys locate a well-concealed and disturbingly large diamondback rattlesnake. We pay the usual respects and forage our way home.

August 12, Monday

Sitting with my coffee in the morning darkness, I listen to turkeys softly chattering on their roosting limbs. As the eastern sky begins to glow a faint amber, the turkeys acknowledge their anticipation with louder vocalizations, the strongest of which, when heard at a distance, might be called a tree yelp.

The sky becomes saturated with brilliant horizontal bands of crimson. I sit in the near darkness, my back to this spectacle, and watch as our world is slowly illuminated. The turkeys, encouraged by my presence, one by one drop to the ground around me. Some stretch their wings and do their strange little dance, a joyful, happy dance, expressing an exuberance that I do not share at this moment. Some gather around me—they stand close at eye level—and in the semidarkness, their eyes are wet and dark. The red glow of the sunrise is reflected in their eyes and appears to me as a fiery projection coming from within. There is a fire in these birds, an ancient flame that has transcended time. It shines on me and I can feel its warmth. In spite of my slumbering humanity, there is something combustible within me, and I can feel some pale smoldering ember begin to burn brighter. These young birds are an inspiration, and in some way I am empowered by them— the primal totemic relationship. As humans, we have struck an evolutionary bargain that has left us desolate, isolated, and consumed by a cold darkness born of our peculiar consciousness, a chill from which we can find few places of refuge or solace. I am bathed in the warm glow of these extraordinary creatures.

This morning I will be a man in search of a grasshopper. It is a calling as strong as any I have ever known. Perhaps I am onto something.

We raid the field like ancient marauding barbarians. Grasshoppers may speak of this day with a shudder for generations to come. Arriving at the northern end of the field, we find the sun dancing through the hammock onto the wet scrub of the field. Crows herald our arrival, and quail share our exuberance. Even the noisy red-shouldered hawk that has intimidated us all summer seems to keep his distance in respect. This morning we are the definition of environmental impact.

We move into the hammock around midmorning, and the mood changes completely. A quiet area overlooking Bert's Branch affords us a couple of hours of relaxed and quiet browsing. We listen to bird sounds. A family of pileated woodpeckers works over a dead water oak very near to us, and the turkeys are fascinated by their noisy activity. We observe one of these large woodpeckers at close range as she hunts for grubs in the base of the dead oak. Drawing her head back, she slams her bill one time into the rotting bark with an audible hollow thud. Then delicately she places her ear close to the bark and listens intently for a second or two. Moving up the side of the tree a few inches, she repeats her singular attack and once again listens carefully. This procedure is repeated until at last her blow apparently produces some audible movement within the soft wood of the tree, and then with a great resounding blur of pounding blows she sends a small cloud of wood chips and dust showering to the ground. She exposes a large, plump white beetle larva, seizes it, and with one confident gulp, it disappears. We watch in silent wonder.

Acknowledging our presence, a deer blows at us seventy-five yards up the creek. The turkeys afford him their undivided attention for some time.

As predicted, storms approach from the southwest. We return home in the afternoon. The turkeys are particularly insistent on my presence, so I remain with them until lightning forces me inside. They fly up on the roost.

I have been wearing camouflage while sitting in the hammock in an effort to have less impact on the turkeys' surroundings. They have been rather unaccepting of it, however, and try occasionally to remove it. They still would prefer my blue uniform.

As I sit quietly against the base of a tree, the turkeys will now, on occasion, wander quite far away, foraging. Through the open woods of the hammock, I see them feeding along, not at all unlike similar flocks of wild turkeys I have observed in the past. At this distance I know that their experience and interaction with the surrounding environment is unaffected by my presence. I see that the land is what they know and understand—it is what they are. If I were to suddenly disappear, they would gracefully melt into all of this like the palmettos and pine trees. Clearly, they are perfectly interwoven into the most subtle and beautiful fabric of this landscape. I feel that one day soon the need to be with me will be outweighed by the desire to forge ahead on their own, and, possibly without ever looking back, they will be gone. But for now, as long as they want to be with me, I will remain as close to them as my life will permit. One day soon I know I will walk home alone.

August 14, Wednesday

Arriving at the pen at first light, I find that everyone is well and ready to get started. Rain is forecast for the entire day, so we spend as much time as possible vigorously raiding the grasslands and the scrub. The temperature is pleasant, the gnats are not a bother, and we do not slow down. Insects and seeds are in abundance, and we try to consume as much as possible before the rains come.

The sweet, meaty fruits of summer are quickly disappearing, and signs of the coming autumn are everywhere. Grasses, particularly broom grass (*Andropogon*), are beginning to grow tall and will be topping out soon. Liatris and deer tongue, although not yet in bloom, are sending up tall spikes everywhere. Likewise, the partridge pea, or *Cassia*, is well developed, and today I see its first yellow flowers showing around the field. Soon the old field will be alive with rich hues of purple and yellow. The white to pink to red, color-transcendent trailing legume (*Tephrosia spicata*) continues to bloom residually about, along with the pale meadow beauty (*Rhexia mariana*). Yellow-eyed grass (*Xyris* sp.) still blooms here and there, but much of it has gone to seed cone. Pawpaw (*Asimina angustifolia*), which grows abundantly in the area, has gone to seed and is laden with the cocoons of next season's zebra swallowtails. Various species of woody hypericum grow in different parts of the field, and their bright yellow flowers may be seen all about. Occasional stands of winged sumac (*Rhus copellina*), which dot the field, are now in flower. The trailing legumes centrosema and clitoria are blooming around the margins of the field. The sweet green pods of *Crotalaria sagittalis,* so popular with the turkeys all summer, have become hard and black. The yearning turkeys can be heard mouthing the noisy pods but no longer seem to eat them. Beggar lice (*Desmodium* sp.) are about, and the turkeys will not allow these sticky and desirable seeds to remain on my jeans or boots. Clumps of false foxglove (*Agalinis purpurea*) are appearing in the field but will not bloom until September. Another sure sign of autumn is the white *Eupatorium serontinum,* which precedes its lavender relative ageratum by a few weeks. The golden aster (*Pityopsis graminifolia*) is abundant in the south end of the field and is beginning to bloom now. Soon the field will glow uniformly with these small delicate yellow flowers.

Around the damp margin of the hammock, the swamp sunflowers (*Helianthus angustifolius*) are beginning to bud—the physical argument for the direct unimpeded conversion of sunlight into matter, they assault the eye as profoundly as thunder assaults the ear. It is a well-known biological phenomenon: The human mind will not function while staring at a patch of sunlit swamp sunflowers, and facial muscles are gradually subverted into the display of an involuntary smile. Human consciousness is quickly and mercifully undone by the overwhelming vision of so much perfection.

The field is wet from much rain and a heavy dew. It is not too surprising then that we encounter a grumpy snapping turtle in the upper field, far from any real water. The turkeys are not particularly impressed or interested, and we allow him to proceed relatively undisturbed.

As midday approaches, storms send us heading for home. We encounter resident wild turkeys in an overgrown area of the field, who I am sure see me but also see and hear these turkeys. Although I cannot see the strangers, these turkeys begin an interesting conversation with them that consists of some loud putting. I notice that the voices of the two groups are indistinguishable except by the forty or fifty yards that separate us. I don't observe any desire in these turkeys to join the strangers. As lightning begins to strike nearby, we quickly move toward home. Several trees have been struck and killed in the old field this summer.

By now most of the turkeys have fowl pox but, with the exception of unsightly sores on their faces and heads, seem unaffected. I worry about secondary infections, however. Understanding that fowl pox is a part of every wild turkey's experience that simply must run its course, it consoles me somehow that the strangers we have just encountered may be having the same difficulties. Misery loves company.

We have been encountering other wild turkeys almost every day since we began our outings, although I am usually only made aware of this by the behavior and vocalization of my companions. Most of the time the group sees or hears the strangers and I do not, and normally, of course, the resident wild turkeys have also seen me. I have observed the residents' obvious confusion about our odd association on a few occasions. In any case, I know that I have prevented direct interaction between these turkeys and the residents. I am anxious for that to occur and hope the camouflage clothes will help make it possible. I feel certain it is only a matter of time before a little luck will afford us the experience.

August 16, Friday

We have a productive but strenuous outing up through the old field. The gnats are distracting today, and we have difficulty ignoring them.

A beautiful pygmy rattlesnake is on his way across the field. Appearing very purplish against a mat of dead grasses and pine straw, he watches the turkeys carefully as they gather around, alternately studying and jeering. The snake does not seem to take offense at the inquisition, and the turkeys soon join me as I move on.

August 17, Saturday

Today is a big workday around Wren Nest, and I spend the day doing chores in the rain. It is wet and humid, and the gnats are bothersome, so we don't go out today. I still manage to find occasional opportunities to sit with the birds while the rain falls.

August 18, Sunday

Compensating for yesterday, we start out early and heavily browse the old field. The turkeys are excited about the day and waste no time in remembering how to be wild turkeys.

They always appear to be perfectly contented in the pen and never complain about being there. They never pace the fence or want out except when I am near and they try to join me. They relax and indulge in various activities such as dusting, preening, and mock aggressive behaviors. I can, however, sense a great relief in them immediately upon leaving the pen. They are very patient and somehow have an ability to suspend and suppress their desire to be out. Wild turkeys do spend a large part of their time in the wild resting and involving themselves with the activities I observe in the pen. But while in the pen I am certain that they are missing a stimulation that they need and enjoy. I feel guilty if they miss a single day's outing.

Turkey pox is evident on almost everyone, although the amount of involvement seems to vary greatly from one individual to the next. A couple of the turkeys look quite pitiful, with sores over much of their heads, whereas others have only one or two small sores. The malady is primarily cosmetic, it seems, and everyone appears to feel well.

Plumage is looking very adult now. Few juvenile feathers remain, the most obvious ones being the more proximal tertiary flight feathers and one row of upper secondary coverts bordering the beautiful greater secondary coverts. I can now distinguish the resident wild turkeys' tracks in many cases because most are smaller than any made by these turkeys.

After foraging through the field for a couple of hours, we move into the hammock to escape the heat. I arrive at Bert's Branch ahead of the turkeys just as a hooded warbler flies up from the bed of the creek and alights a couple of steps in front of me on a small branch. He is indifferent to my presence and busily scans an adjacent wax myrtle limb for insects.

Hooded warblers are not uncommon in these old-growth hard-wood forests. Solitary, retiring, they prefer quiet damp places, and are extremely difficult to observe. Few people see one in a lifetime. Their curious habit is to repeatedly spread their dark greenish tails with a quick flashing motion, briefly exposing bright white spots on either side. Occasionally, by staring blankly into the hammock, one may be spotted, like a small flashbulb, busily feeding along in the dense under-story vegetation or close to the ground. Their active habits make them nearly impossible to study for long periods, but when a rare opportunity arises to observe these shy birds at close range, they are found to be impossibly beautiful.

The male is pale yellow below, with contrasting olive green back and tail. Covering the head, neck, and upper breast is a uniform, light-absorbent black unsurpassed in its richness in all of nature. Centered in this absolute vacuum of observable light is a mask of shocking brilliant yellow—like the sun seen through a hole in a dark box. Two small black glassy pearls stare out from their golden pool. Unable to avert my eyes in the presence of the supernatural, I always stare in wonder.

Many times I have seen a hummingbird confront the warbler, who usually surrenders the area to the much smaller aggressor. The hummer then typically chases after the larger bird, and both quickly disappear into the distance. With this sole exception, I never see hummers in hostile pursuit outside of their own species. Observing this phenomenon many times over the years and knowing hummingbirds to be generally pugnacious, I have always wondered what could be found so specifically objectionable about the hooded warbler.

Recently, while observing a hooded warbler desperately trying to ignore a hummingbird's aggressive antics displayed directly in his face, it occurred to me at last that I have, for years, failed to see the obvious. Not aggressive at all, the hummer is simply mistaking the warbler for the most brilliant of flowers.

After some brief prospecting and foraging, we find one of our favorite spots overlooking the branch and spend the middle part of the day relaxing. The turkeys sit calmly observing and listening, some wandering slowly about. They let me know when it is time to move on.

Eventually we work our way down the branch, staying close to the run of the stream and crossing back and forth as the terrain dictates. A fresh track from a young black bear has been left on a small sandbar, accompanied by deer, raccoon, and now wild turkey. I avoid stepping on the bar and so degrading the integrity of this interesting record of activity. Human footprints, I find, are always a disappointment in the wilderness, even when they are my own.

As I sit quietly against a tree, a pair of red-shouldered hawks moves in. Obviously attracted to the activity of the turkeys, the hawks begin to make me uncomfortable. The turkeys are scattered down the creek from me, in the direction of the hawks, and are, of course, alert to these aspiring predators. A hawk moves in close, and I fear a panic is about to occur. I give an alarm purr and am surprised when the turkeys take no evasive action and make no attempt to hide. With tails spread wide and feathers fluffed, they stand their ground, displaying a behavior I have observed and photographed many times in adult wild turkeys. The turkeys are growing up, and I can breathe a little easier now. These hawks have been badgering us all summer, but we, at last, have outgrown them. The dejected hawks, pursued by jays, finally make a noisy retreat.

Gradually wandering out of the hammock in the direction of home, we find a freshly dropped secondary flight feather from an adult wild turkey. It is in good condition, although it shows normal wear from having been in service for one year. We proceed and encounter another pygmy rattlesnake, which receives little more than an obligatory acknowledgment. While browsing the old field, we again encounter the dead gopher tortoise that we have visited occasionally all summer. The carapace is starting to weather, so I decide to add it to my turtle shell collection.

We arrive home after what feels like a very full day. Typically we cover distances on our walks that I estimate to be in the range of two to three miles. This distance is compounded considerably by the zigzag pattern of foraging as we laterally visit food plants and chase insects. For every mile I walk, the turkeys have probably walked and run two. Generally, when we arrive home, we look and feel as though we have had a strenuous workout. Heat, humidity, and the strain of ever-present insects also take their toll on us.

August 19, Monday

The skies are disturbed this morning, and rain is predicted. We move into the field with the hope of completing a good outing before the storms begin. The temperature is pleasant, the gnats are not bad, and grasshoppers are abundant.

Yesterday, I dropped the adult turkey feather I had just found as I collected the gopher tortoise shell. Today we gradually forage our way back to retrieve it, and I arrive at the site a minute or two ahead of the turkeys. The feather and the largest pygmy rattlesnake I have ever seen are lying among a few remaining turtle bones looking like the ingredients of some mystic brew. I stare at this odd conjunction and feel that I am only a tourist in some foreign realm—I can see the signs, but I do not know what they mean. The snake nervously flicks his tail as I examine him. The spell is broken, and he quickly crawls to the cover of a nearby wax myrtle bush just before the first turkey arrives. I grab the feather, and the turkeys stir around in the turtle bones. We respectfully ignore the rattlesnake and continue on our way up the field. As if to complete the effect, thunder rumbles in the distance.

Highbush gallberries are ripening just as the last of the deer berries dry on the ground. They are numerous on the west side of the old field, and we find a dense thicket loaded with fruit. A small native holly, the gallberry produces a glossy fruit that is soft, plump, and juicy—the size of a blueberry but almost black in color. I find that they have a nearly undetectable sweetness, not as tart as deer berries, and a slightly bitter aftertaste reminiscent of oversteeped tea. I sample a few and decide that gallberries, like grasshoppers, are principally wild turkey food. I am reduced once again from participant to mere observer. The turkeys, accustomed to fresh berries all summer, have become hungry for fruit and disappear into the thick cover, eating their fill. They become quite noisy as they enthusiastically pluck as many berries as they can hold. One by one they leave the gallberry patch and, with uniformly purple mouths, join me in the field.

We forage across the southern border of the national forest, flushing a small covey of quail. The turkeys watch attentively but are not startled, obviously wondering what all the fuss is about. It is good to see young quail. Due to a lack of controlled burning, they have been on the decline here for years.

Storms are pressing from the southwest. The wind begins to blow, and we head as directly as possible for home.

I have had various experiences with the imprinting process in wild animals. The list includes pocket gophers, cotton rats, flying squirrels, gray squirrels, fox squirrels, gray foxes, red foxes, coyotes, bobcats, raccoons, possums, white-tailed deer, various primates, wood ducks, quail, crows, numerous songbirds, hawks, owls, and to some extent a variety of reptiles, which do not seem really to imprint on anything except maybe food. I have always considered that the best way to know a wild animal's true nature is by sharing your bed with it. I have been lucky to live in places where they could share my world and still never have to leave their own—although I know for a fact that, given a choice, a raccoon will always prefer a warm bed and a pecan sandy to a hollow log and a frog.

This particular experience with these wild turkeys has been unique for me in that I have never attempted to keep an imprinted animal's experience so completely insulated from my own. I do not want them to share my life but instead defer to theirs as much as possible. Attempting to do what they do, go where they would go, and even speak their language, I have been very careful to keep them isolated from my world. They have never been into the yard or near the cabin, for example. They see my truck from a distance but have never been close to it. We go directly from the pen to the field and directly back. They have never encountered another human being while on an outing, not even Claudia. I never feed them directly from my hand. I want to experience their true nature with as little human influence as possible. We have been extremely lucky, admittedly, and this experiment has already surpassed all of my expectations.

For most of my life I have observed, painted, drawn, hunted, read about, photographed, and generally studied the wild turkey. Entering this current relationship with many preconceived notions, I did not expect to find that I had misunderstood so much. In spite of an enormous respect and admiration for the bird, I had managed to underestimate its complexity.

That wild turkeys are clever and wily is a cliché among hunters and people who have had any experience with them. No one comes to terms with this phenomenon more often than the turkey hunter. A turkey's sensory ability clearly borders on the supernatural.

I am astounded by the wild turkey's ability to determine distance and direction and I have learned that a spring gobbler who answers my call from a quarter of a mile away needs no other sound from me. If he chooses to come, he will know almost exactly from what bush or tree trunk the call came. Even through dense terrain, I have had turkeys come on the run from such a distance and stop within twenty yards, then begin examining my exact location for the source of the yelp.

Vision in wild turkeys, although very acute, as Lovett Williams points out, may be no better than human vision. Where wild turkeys excel is in their ability to detect movement. They apparently can discern (in a fully animated world) the smallest movement. A tiny flicker of motion fifty yards away gets their attention like a slap in the face. This ability seems especially developed in regard to motion overhead. I spend a large portion of my time with these young turkeys trying to figure out what they have just seen or heard. Often when I find out, I am astonished.

Hearing is acute in wild turkeys, although it is difficult to study. I do find, however, that sounds in general, although never ignored, may be tolerated, provided they do not have dangerous associations. The turkeys are perfectly comfortable with a chainsaw as long as it, like the noisy red-shouldered hawk, remains in the distance.

I have experimented with odd noises sounded from a blind while photographing wild turkeys. Often, when exposed to the most ridiculous noises, a wild turkey will listen and attempt to observe the origin of the sound; if no alarming association can be made, he will gradually begin to ignore it. Wild turkeys can be very attentive to camera noises for a short time, but if the photographer is completely concealed, the sounds will eventually be ignored. One sure way to disturb or frighten wild turkeys, ironically, is with a turkey caller. They seem very limited in their tolerance for meaningless yelping. They usually regard the human voice as something to be feared as well.

Everything that I have observed regarding the sensory abilities of these imprinted wild turkeys has impressed me with how profound these attributes are. When in the turkeys' presence, I feel dull and insensitive by comparison. Frequently, I experience genuine embarrassment as I have occasion to make my ignorance and stupidity known to them in some way. Sometimes I get collective looks that I can only interpret as incredulity.

It has always been my impression that wild turkeys rely principally on instinct and profound sensory acuity for survival and adaptation. Two things have surprised me, however. One is how elaborate and complete inherited information is in wild turkeys, and the other is that they do have well-developed cognitive abilities. It appears that wild turkeys begin with a genetic program of adaptive information and then set about gathering the details specific to their particular environment. Every day I see that the most important activity of a young wild turkey is the acquisition and assimilation of information. It is the food they are most hungry for. They are curious to a fault, they want a working understanding of every aspect of their surroundings, and their memory is impeccable. They gather specific information about a particular environment, conspicuously apply that information to a framework of general knowledge, and make appropriate choices in modifying their behavior. The apologies that precede discussions about wild turkey intelligence are definitely not warranted. I have never observed another animal making such a dedicated effort to know and to understand.

Turkeys in general are often regarded as relatively unintelligent and even wildlife biologists occasionally express reservations about wild turkey intellect. But an interesting comparison can be made with a presumption that frequently is made about the common crow.

People often consider the crow to be particularly sharp-witted, perhaps recognizing traits that are all too familiar. Crows are gregarious, noisy, seemingly arrogant, fascinated by bright colors and objects that sparkle, and we may unconsciously see ourselves mirrored in their behavior. I have imprinted and raised crows, both individually and in groups, and observed that they are indeed clever, displaying behaviors that imply innate curiosity, a well-developed social organization, a vocabulary of sorts, et cetera. In comparing the two species directly, however, I have to concede that, along with many other distinctions, wild turkeys display more curiosity than crows, are much more complex socially, and have a more complicated vocabulary. And so, upon a closer but admittedly subjective examination, the wild turkey simply appears more highly developed and intelligent than the crow.

August 21, Wednesday

A record low temperature for this date is set today at 61 degrees. It is wonderful, and at first light we are in the field witnessing a glorious orange sunrise. We owe the cool front to Hurricane Bob in the Atlantic and our brilliant sunrise to Mount Pinatubo in the Philippines. We shall not overanalyze our good fortune, however, and will be merely grateful that nature can be so baroque.

A heavy dew makes the land wet, and we leave temporary meandering trails in the grass as we aggressively forage the old field. Grasshoppers are flightless and vulnerable in the dampness of early morning, and we capitalize. As the first sunlight breaks through the tree line of the hammock to the east, we have already had a productive browse through the field. Tails are wet. The jewel-like beads of water standing on the turkeys' backs seem somehow redundant against the iridescent bronzes, blues, and greens of their plumage.

Before the sun has risen above the tree line we quietly slip into the cool, misty shadows of the hammock. We cross the branch, and, as I settle against a young water oak overlooking the creek and a beautiful open area of the hammock, the turkeys contentedly wander, exploring and gathering food. They seem stimulated and are more vocal than usual.

After only a few minutes in the hammock we are startled by wild turkey noise that is not our own. We hear faint putts and yelps in the thick bay area just below us on the creek. The turkeys become more and more interested in the activity downstream, and some begin to head slowly in the strangers' direction with heads raised.

A wild turkey with a smooth, musical, constantly repeated yelp is moving in our direction, apparently attracted by the continuous purrs, putts, and trills she hears up the branch. Now two other turkeys are slowly moving in our direction. They respond to us with *pit, pit*. I hear turkeys flying in the hammock seventy-five yards farther down the creek, and there is more yelping in the bay swamp; we are with a significant number of resident wild turkeys.

The three turkeys below us move up the creek as several of our turkeys walk down. They converge overlooking the creek twenty-five yards below me. I am strangely nervous—the way I have felt many times before as wild turkeys moved in on me in the woods. It is a tense moment, as the turkeys may interact directly with resident wild turkeys for the first time without my interference. I have imagined all manner of things happening at this moment.

Though we have had interesting vocal exchanges with resident wild turkeys almost daily and have seen them from a distance, there has been no face-to-face interaction. The resident turkeys are aware of my presence, but over the course of the summer, they seem to have become somewhat accepting of it and often now will stay in close proximity even though I am in direct view. It seems that their interest in these turkeys is beginning to outweigh their fear of me. We are the largest flock of wild turkeys in the area, and the residents must find it confusing and curious that these turkeys are constantly in the presence of a man.

The resident wild turkeys are accustomed to meeting strangers on a daily basis and do not consider this particular encounter to be unusual. The three who have come to investigate appear only superficially interested. They quietly feed around and seem unconcerned with direct interaction. Our turkeys are not interested in a confrontation and, although they are completely attentive, exhibit no unusual behavior. Some actually begin to ignore the strangers and go about foraging. I sit like a statue for an hour or so while the strangers browse across the creek. The young turkeys calmly watch and listen to all the wild turkey noise around them and then respond by becoming relatively noisy themselves, although I detect a rather pitiful shyness in them. Suddenly, a fourth resident turkey moves directly in and walks through a gallberry thicket to the edge of the creek. She makes a loud, startling, staccato vocalization that I would describe as a cutting cackle. It causes the other three strangers to move back down the branch and proves very distressing to the young turkeys, who likewise leave the branch and nervously return to me. They are obviously affected by this event and sit close by my side, very still and completely quiet for a long time, cautiously scanning the hammock below us. I am certain that they are listening to wild turkeys that I cannot hear. Eventually, they relax and resume normal behavior, and I assume the strangers have moved out of hearing range. For some reason, I feel a little disappointment for the turkeys and a little angry at the strange turkey for being so rude. It is possible, of course, that the fourth turkey saw me, even though I was wearing camouflage.

Later, we move back across the creek, slowly and carefully foraging along the interior edge of the hammock. As we work our way down and out of the hammock, we notice evidence of much fresh wild turkey activity along the way. I collect a newly shed feather from the alula of an adult wild turkey, and the turkeys peck at numerous smaller body feathers that have been dropped here and there.

We browse the old field in the afternoon and eventually head home in a heat that reminds me that it is still summer.

One of the most interesting and gratifying aspects of this project is observing the absolute joy that these birds experience in their lives. Normally, dealing with human-imprinted wildlife on a day-to-day basis involves inevitable frustrations as a particular species' nature will, sooner or later, come into conflict with the unnatural effect of association with the human environment.

I observe no such frustration in these birds, and they appear to enjoy every aspect of their lives. They constantly express an enthusiasm and a dignified excitement that cause me to feel very optimistic about our overall approach. Whether foraging the hammock, browsing the old field, or returning to the roost and entering the pen, these young wild turkeys are always exuberant and completely devoted to the moment. It is as though they would change nothing—they are in love with being alive. We never experience a situation or a moment in the day in which their participation is not completely willing. I honestly don't know how to account for it. To share in this is a great reward for me.

August 22, Thursday

Another cool and pleasant morning. The gnats seem to have subsided at long last, although they still are present. The cool weather is accompanied by a lack of rain, which allows us to spend the entire day aggressively involved in our various wild turkey activities.

Retreating to the hammock at midday, we spend time relaxing by the branch. The cooler weather inspires the turkeys to explore, and so we work up the west side of the creek. We enter some thick areas consisting of bay swamp bordered by thickets of wild azalea, gallberry, dog hobble, summer titi, black titi, and viburnum. Very relaxed, the birds browse slowly, as if they have no destination in mind. While visiting some new territory, they locate an old terra-cotta turpentine pot that has somehow avoided breakage in this hidden recess of the hammock. They quickly determine that although interesting, it is not a wild turkey thing, and we all seem to silently agree that its secret repose will be safe with us. A well-hidden box turtle nearby seems to share an abstract kinship with the pot, as well as a solitude that we have temporarily interrupted.

We have not encountered a snake of any kind for the last couple of days, which is unusual. I think a few days of dry weather must be responsible.

Evidence of resident wild turkey activity is common in many areas of the hammock. I find another adult secondary flight feather to add to the collection. Viburnum berries (*Viburnum nudum*), known locally as possum haw, are ripe, and though they are not abundant, the turkeys find them agreeable. Palmetto berries are likewise darkening, and the turkeys browse on them from time to time. Fox grapes are not very common in the area, but where they do occur close to the ground, they provide a substantial source of fruit. Grasses are going to seed everywhere, but the more popular ones have been heavily browsed by the resident wild turkeys. One species in particular, a so-called panic grass (*Panicum rigidulum*), appears to be an important food for the turkeys. Panicum is a large and complicated genus. Many domestic millets are derived from this group. We find also that we are competing with the residents for the few remaining deer berries and blueberries. Everyone knows the locations of the bushes that are bearing fruit. The foxes in the area are also browsing these shrubs; I see their tracks and droppings regularly. Some of these bushes are beginning to look quite abused from all the competitive foraging.

August 23, Friday

We return home at midday in the rain, allowing plenty of time for a late afternoon outing. I return to the cabin and decide to have a quick meal while the rain is falling. The rain and the meal take about thirty minutes. As I sit on the porch, putting my boots back on, I look up and see in the yard a large, red Doberman pinscher. Jumping up, I grab a running shoe and chase after him, missing him with the shoe. He bolts into the field and heads north.

Running to the pen, I find the turkeys standing around limp and bloody. They pant and wander slowly about as if in a daze, with their wings hanging loose. Seeing a hen lying still in the corner, I go over to her and sadly discover that she is dead. There is a small wire cut on her head, but she appears otherwise unhurt. Judging by the dent in the wire above her, she flew into the side of the pen at a high rate of speed. Perhaps she broke her neck or bled internally.

The pen, I realize now, is no longer an ally. It was constructed to exclude everything from possums to bears, but it cannot exclude the turkeys' inherent wildness. Even though the dog was unable to enter the pen, the turkeys have nearly destroyed themselves with explosive bursts of flight. Their powerful flight, coupled now with the substantial weight of their bodies, has made the pen a deadly hazard.

With the exception of the dead hen, the young males seem to have fared the worst. Their heavier bodies have made their escape efforts more destructive. All the males have multiple abrasions on their bills and heads. Two are having trouble standing and are shaky when they try to walk. One little hen whom I call Sweet Pea, already slightly sick with fowl pox, now looks very stressed. I fear that two or three more could die. I am heartbroken.

I immediately add medication to their water and begin examining each turkey individually. Thankfully, there are no broken bones, but everyone has cuts and abrasions, and I worry about internal injuries. I can only sit with them and wait. After the initial shock of the event subsides, the turkeys all want to lie around close to me and sleep. Darkness is approaching, and I worry that they will be unable to fly up on the roost.

I bury the dead hen in one of the brown towels that she was hatched on and sit with the survivors until darkness surrounds us. Three are unable to fly up on the roost—Sweet Pea and two jakes, Turkey Boy and Starker.

After dark, it begins to rain steadily, and our misery seems to be complete. Several hours later, I make sure the three grounded turkeys are under the dry roof and go inside. I check on them several times during the night and with each visit expect to find another dead turkey, but I do not.

August 24, Saturday

Understandably, the turkeys all look and act very poorly today, wanting only to lie around sleeping. Several are limping, but the bloody faces have dried up, improving their appearance somewhat. Sweet Pea seems to be doing fairly well. Beautiful Samara has a nasty deep gash on the top of her head.

We spend the entire day recovering in the pen. Everyone is very nervous. I have decided that as soon as the turkeys are completely recovered, they must begin living and roosting outside the pen. We cannot risk another incident. We have all come too far.

By evening I feel that the rest of the turkeys will survive; none apparently has grave injuries. I remain vigilant for the dog. None of the neighbors knows of such a dog in the area, but everyone is in agreement that he must be destroyed if he returns. I hope he will not.

August 25, Sunday

The turkeys appear to be improved this morning, although they are still sluggish and sleepy. The weather is stormy, so it is a good day to continue to rest and recover. The turkeys' mood seems to be one of depression and resignation. I cannot help but feel the same.

I have a great sense of loss over the hen who was killed; I feel as though I have lost a friend. I relate to each of the turkeys in different and special ways. They are very individual, and each of their spirits is unique. This entire experience has verified an observation I have made many times over the years, that wild turkeys vary in personality from one individual to the next. Such variation could account for much of the unpredictable behavior that we observe in turkeys in the wild. As any turkey hunter will attest, only a small percentage of wild turkeys behave and respond in a predictable manner.

The rains subside in the afternoon, and I feel we are ready for a short, relaxing outing. As we leave the pen, there is no energetic burst of flight but rather an orderly procession out to the edge of the field. As we move into the dampness of the green land, like the clouds, a darkness is lifted from our spirits. In a short time we begin to recall who we are and put our pains behind us—sore muscles are stretched and loosened—tension gradually disappears along with the thunderheads. Their voices return and so do their appetites—our attention soon turns to crickets and crotalaria, grasshoppers and gallberries, partridge peas and argiopes.

The turkeys surround and greet a resentful black racer. Later, we chase a large rattlesnake into a gopher tortoise burrow and, after considerable jeering into the damp blackness of the cavity, mock him by dusting away his tracks. It seems as though we have risen from our ashes. The fire has been rekindled.

August 26, Monday

The weather is nasty, with thunderstorms beginning early. The turkeys are very well recovered today from their ordeal, and I am grateful that things did not turn out much worse.

The last juvenile tail feather molted today from one of the hens. I actually photographed the event. A few of the central first-basic tail feathers are likewise beginning to fall, indicating they are beginning the partial molt known as the prealternate molt, according to Lovett Williams. Following the completion of this molt, the wild turkey has acquired its "first winter plumage." A very few juvenile contour feathers remain. These beautiful birds would now appear to any untrained observer to be fully grown wild turkeys.

August 27, Tuesday

I am anxious to take the turkeys out, but thunderstorms are about, so we must wait. It is late when the rains subside, but it is important to go out if only for a short walk. The afternoon is cool following the rain, and we are all enthusiastic. Immediately hitting the field, we begin browsing and manage to reach midway before realizing that the sun will set soon. Starting directly home and feeling much better than before, we arrive at the pen just before dark.

I enter the pen, but, curiously, the turkeys for the first time fail to follow me. It is as though they have reached a consensus prior to returning to the pen. They begin limb chatter and wander around eyeing the trees, and within moments the first turkey flies up into a nearby

pine. With a great deal of chatter, others begin flying up into the surrounding trees. Limbing behavior, precedent to roosting, lasts until
nearly dark, and they gradually begin to settle down in the upper
reaches of the tall pines.

The birds always seem to let me know the right time and place
for things, making it easy for me. They have never once hesitated to
follow me into the pen, and I have been worrying how to make this
transition, but they, once again it seems, have made the decision.

As I sit, watching and listening, they settle in for the night. Sil-
houettes of turkeys dot the surrounding pines against the night sky as
they spread out, two or three turkeys to a tree. One jake wanders the
ground until nearly dark, finally deciding on a tree bordering the field,
quite far from the others. Seeing heads bobbing slowly against the
darkened sky and hearing faint putts and trills, I am reminded of some
cold winter evening, as a boy, observing a similar flock of wild turkeys
on the roost in anticipation of the next day's hunt.

I try to recall whether in my young mind, at that moment, I could
have imagined, anticipated, or even longed for the irony of the present
moment and this strange continuity. Like an arrow shot high and
blind, it seems as though I have traveled very far although my path was
peregrine. It appears, in retrospect, that my trajectory could only have
brought me eventually to this singular experience. I realize now that
as a young hunter, my intent was not merely to kill for food this elusive bird, but was rather my clumsy way of reaching toward something
that enchanted and mystified me.

After night has completely fallen and the turkeys have grown
quiet, I give a very soft lost call, and they respond and reassure me that
no one, with the possible exception of myself, is lost. I am confident
that they are safe but feel a little strange, as though I have been left
out. This is one wild turkey activity in which I cannot participate. The
waning moon is still large, and I can imagine that their first night
roosted high in the trees will be exciting and liberating for them. Later,
as the moon begins to show through the tree line to the east, I move
slowly toward the cabin.

Standing in a great expanse of old-growth longleaf pine, open and clean, I realize that overhead I am covered by a large, exposed-beam roof. There are no walls, as in some open-air conference center or one of those New Age, nondenominational churches. I observe that the ground and vegetation beneath this structure are natural and undisturbed. Judging by the angle of the light and the mist reaching out over the wiregrass and scattered palmettos, it must be early morning. With a penetrating feeling of remoteness and solitude, I look up to see a large flock of adult wild turkeys moving in around me. I remain motionless and stunned as they casually feed and browse nearby. Though they seem to ignore me, I sense that these unfamiliar individuals are silently acknowledging my presence. An elegant hen passes very close, and I cannot help but ask, "Are you human imprinted?"

Seemingly pleased that I would inquire, she answers in a refined and articulate voice, "No, we are not human imprinted."

I hesitate, but then shyly mention, "I'm sure you don't know who I am, but I was involved with a large family of human-imprinted wild turkeys."

The hen seems to glow and then looks deep within my eyes and says warmly, "Oh, we know who you are."

Glancing back affectionately, she rejoins the flock as they wander away feeding in the crisp morning air.

I awaken feeling deeply touched and honored, having received the greatest of compliments, and simultaneously worry that I may have completely lost my mind. Henry Thoreau once said, "Our truest life is when we are in dreams awake."

August 28, Wednesday

The early morning darkness finds me sipping a cup of coffee that I cannot see. The temperature is unusually warm, and I am wrapped in a dark, vaporous blanket; my cup is full of this stuff, and I drink it down.

Sitting on the wet ground beneath the turkeys, my small pack laden with food and gear to sustain me for the coming day, I can hear sleepy putts from the surrounding trees as the first blush of light finally brightens the eastern sky. Slowly the field becomes illuminated. The turkeys respond with excited noises, and they begin flying from limb to limb. Moving into the lower edge of the field, seventy-five yards from the roost, I yelp softly three times, and the turkeys, with a great clatter, begin flying from the tops of the trees. The blue morning air is filled with wild turkeys, some alighting around me and others passing close to my head at velocities that are frightening.

Scattered at first across the open area of the lower field, we eventually merge. They have definitely had a more restful night than I.

The sun is not yet near the horizon, and the heavy dewfall causes the wet vegetation of the field to gather light like a winter frost. The turkeys seem to react by becoming very quiet and observant. They wander slowly about, their legs appearing long as they hold their breast feathers tight and their tails far from the wet grass.

The tattered remains of spiderwebs are everywhere, hanging like jeweled garlands over grass and limb, looking like the remnants of some sinister celebration. They hang in the stillness of the dawn. The turkeys appear to regard all of this with a certain respectful solemnity. For them, there is a nourishment in all of this that is more profound than hunger.

Our gradual progress up the open center of the field is monitored from the upper end by one of the large bucks that we have seen occasionally all summer. At a hundred yards, he looks very blue and almost transparent against the dark backdrop of thick young pines. His branching antlers glow, appearing unusually narrow and tall as the velvet gathers light reflected from the wet ground. He stares intently like a pale monarch with a gossamer crown, a diaphanous surveyor of a great, jeweled hall. I squint at the buck with my tired eyes and realize that he has vanished. We wander eventually to the spot where the big deer stood, and I see where he turned and moved away. His steps are broad and deliberate but not running. His hooves are large and spread slightly in the dark wet sand. I feel a kind of residual heat when I look at the fresh tracks, like some lingering olfactory resonance that would cause the heart of a hound to race.

Sunlight touches the tops of the trees. The turkeys remember to eat.

We deliberately forage the west side of the old field and find that our ripening patch of gallberries has been discovered by others and browsed heavily. Persistence prevails, however, and we manage to root out a few. Lowbush gallberries in other parts of the field are heavy with green berries and promise to be a good source of fruit in the near future.

As soon as the sun tops the tree line we find ourselves ducking from one shady spot to the next. It will be very hot today, so we head in the direction of the hammock. The turkeys have missed the cool darkness of the hammock and soon find a comfortable spot to relax.

A red-shouldered hawk once again moves in aggressively. The turkeys show alarm but do not panic, repeating their defiant behavior with tails spread wide. The hawk makes several passes through the trees, alighting in different places to take a close look at us. I remain very still in camouflage clothing. As the hawk observes the turkeys from thirty yards away, I experiment with the alarm purr, and the turkeys ignore it completely, not letting their attention stray from the hawk. The hawk observes us briefly and then flies away. The turkeys relax—I relax.

A pair of oven birds visits us for a short time; disturbed by our presence, they scold us repeatedly. Eventually, the strange little birds drop to the ground and walk off through the woods, appearing themselves like small strutting turkeys.

Remembering our previous encounter, the turkeys are now more conscious of the potential presence of other wild turkeys and remain vigilant for them, scanning the surrounding forest with sight and hearing. I watch as they slowly wander to the edge of the branch and carefully scan the bay swamp below us. We see fresh evidence of wild turkeys, including an adult primary flight feather and a small primary covert feather.

Our only reptile encounter is with a black racer, which the turkeys choose to ignore. The racers rarely attempt to run from the turkeys but usually stand their ground. Ordinarily, it would be difficult for me to observe certain snakes closely, as many are inclined to flee when a human comes near. Particularly, the faster snakes like racers and coach whips are prone to take advantage of their speed at such times. When approached by wild turkeys, however, these same snakes almost never run but rather become defensive or belligerent. This phenomenon has made things interesting for me, as I am ignored by these snakes that are concerned with so much undivided attention from the turkeys. As a result I am permitted to observe at close range species that I would otherwise have to either chase down or watch disappear quickly into the distance.

August 29, Thursday

We make another early start. We have put the unnatural effects of the pen behind us. It is a relief for me not to worry about them being trapped in an enclosure, and already the new arrangement is more comfortable for us all. Today is my birthday, and I celebrate with the turkeys, who eat as many grasshoppers as possible in my honor. The old field is very agreeable today—it is a pleasure without the gnats that have plagued us all summer, and we spend more time than usual browsing. A soft breeze blows from the east and the humidity is relatively low, allowing us to forage well into the morning. Today, the sun is our friend.

As we wander into the margin of the hammock, we flush a resident wild turkey at about thirty-five yards; she flies into the bay swamp on upper Bert's Branch. This is the first time we have caused a resident wild turkey to fly. I am sorry our timing couldn't have been a little better.

On arriving at our favorite spot on the branch, we are all ready for a late morning break and set about relaxing. After twenty minutes or so, we begin to hear yelping from the bay swamp a hundred yards to our north. Apparently, the turkey hen was not sufficiently disturbed by us to leave the area. I answer her with some soft putts and yelps. The turkeys are fascinated but cautious and remain motionless and silent. Trying to encourage the hen, I make a faint lost call, which frequently will cause these turkeys to become very vocal, but they respond lightly, and she cannot hear.

The hen moves around us on the opposite side of the branch, vocalizing with constant yelps and occasional sharp inquiring putts. Although I cannot see her, I remain very still, as I am sure she can see us. She walks the thick margin of the hammock—still nervous and wary from our previous awkward encounter.

Finally, she moves back to the north, yelping frequently until out of hearing. The turkeys remain quiet and attentive until eventually all are sound asleep.

August 30, Friday

At first light I have already finished my morning coffee while sitting on the ground beneath the turkeys. I sleep better knowing that the birds rest in the safety of the tall pines. I am greeted by them with an enthusiasm for life that is inspirational.

We are storm-free this afternoon, and it is extremely hot. The turkeys are in a resting mode and are not interested in an adventure but gradually develop some momentum and do some productive foraging. Entering the margin of the hammock, we spend our time out of the sun where the air is cooler.

I lead the turkeys and surprise a large coach whip that rears up, cobralike, from five feet away. His head is eighteen or twenty inches off of the ground; he opens his mouth and literally attacks me. I have to jump back to avoid being bitten on my jeans. Combining this long strike with a break toward a gopher tortoise hole twenty feet away, he disappears. The turkeys miss the entire show. I am grateful that the rattlesnakes generally have a disposition that is more restrained. It would be very unpleasant if they behaved in a similar manner.

Later, as we are working our way back through the field, a hen putts behind me in the unmistakable voice that lets me know a rattlesnake has been found. Most of the others continue foraging ahead, but I go over to take a look. Lying within some thick grass is a one-inch-diameter stick approximately twenty-four inches long and alternately curving. Thinking what a silly mistake for an almost grown wild turkey to make, especially considering the amount of exposure she has had to snakes, I proceed to tell her how silly she is as she continues to alarm putt and crane at the stick. I decide to pull the stick out of the grass to show her how ridiculous she has been and how embarrassed we all are for her. Just as I reach for the stick, something tells me to reconsider. Withdrawing my hand, I peer carefully into the grass, and there within inches of the stick is a rattlesnake in a tight little coil. The hen looks at me and walks away voicing several more putts that sound a little to me like "tsk tsk." I nervously rejoin the group.

A red-shouldered hawk joins us in the hammock again today as we reach the branch. As he settles on an overhanging limb thirty-five yards away and peers admiringly at the turkeys, I stand very still against a tree.

The turkeys seem unconcerned with his intrusion. As an experiment, I begin voicing my old dying mouse routine, which arouses the hawk's curiosity further. He flies to within fifteen yards and perches on a limb almost directly above us. As he nervously bobs his head up and down and back and forth, the turkeys, although alert with some spread tails, are not particularly impressed. The hawk, displaying stoic resignation, gradually begins considering other things. The turkeys continue feeding about and ignore him. I am impressed with how fast these behavioral changes occur. Two weeks ago this would have been a major crisis. Worrying much less about hawk attacks now, I think that great horned owls could still be a threat. Fortunately for these young wild turkeys, horned owls are not common in these woods.

There is much pertaining to my personal experience that I do not write about in these field notes. I write very little about my relationships with the individual turkeys. As I mentioned briefly earlier, wild turkeys do have widely differing and distinct personalities. Appearances among individual turkeys are also diverse, although it is difficult to maintain distinctions due to the fact that young wild turkeys grow and mature so rapidly. An attribute that is conspicuous today may be gone in a short period of time. Certain physical anomalies, of course, like crooked toes and bills that do not perfectly occlude, make identification easy. Often, for immediate recognition, I rely on a particular broken feather or a sore on the head, attributes that may quickly change.

Personality, however, tends to remain very identifiable in each individual. I generally do not like to name wild animals, as it seems somehow demeaning, but I find that it is useful to call these young turkeys by different names since they are so many and I want to be able to have continuity in my observations of individuals. I find myself naming the turkeys by some particular attribute they possess, either a physical or a personality trait.

Even in maturity I can still readily differentiate the two clutches by the variation in the color of the most proximal secondary and tertiary flight feathers. I can also distinguish them by the relative darkness of the tarsus, or lower leg, and by the amount of feathering and coloration on the head—the heads are particularly distinctive.

There was Bright Eyes, who had very peculiar, unusually large eyes. She was also one of three turkeys who developed crooked toes shortly after being born. It would be interesting to know if this is a genetic phenomenon.

Putt Putt made herself conspicuous by being especially vocal and by demanding a lot of attention. She was very affectionate, and her mandibles did not occlude perfectly.

Little Friend also made himself known by his predisposition for closeness. No matter where we were, he would be either directly next to me or in my lap, if I were sitting; I always worried that I might step on him.

Starker is a male from the dark clutch with a crooked outside toe on his left foot. The males now generally display more need for affection and direct interaction than the hens, who are somewhat more independent. He is very much my companion, and although he does not particularly like to be handled, he needs a lot of closeness. He is constantly with me, will sleep in my lap frequently, and can actually be a bother, especially when I am trying to use a camera or write my field notes. He was for a time the largest of all the young turkeys and was always a week or more advanced in plumage development. He is the most handsome of the jakes, although he is no longer the largest, nor is he dominant.

The dominant jake appears to be Rosey, who is the only surviving male from the light clutch. He is slightly larger than the other three males, and his status is no longer in dispute. Most of the aggressive behavior I observe now is among the other three males, who seem to have difficulty establishing who ranks second, third, and fourth. Rosey derives his name from the particularly bright pink caruncles on his head and neck, a trait that he shares somewhat with all of his sisters from the light clutch. The feet and tarsi of this clutch are also very pink as compared to the others. I likewise identify one of his sisters as Rosita; she has particularly bright pink markings on her head and is also very friendly.

If there is real affection in wild turkeys, it is demonstrated most profoundly by Sweet Pea. She is a small hen from the dark clutch who is almost catlike in her need to be held and stroked. If I am sitting, she is in my lap, and she will stay as long as I will let her. She had a hard time with fowl pox, which made her feel bad and also made her feet sore, although she is healthy now. She walks up and presses against me until I make a suitable lap into which she can climb. Even on the hottest day she will insist on being in my lap. Also, her mandibles do not perfectly occlude, giving her an endearing appearance. Sweet Pea is a distraction and consumes a disproportionate amount of my time. I find that her apparent fondness for me instills me with a similar sentiment, and I have to admit that I am particularly attached to her. Her nervous presumption of my complete devotion makes her irresistible.

Samara is a somewhat independent hen from the light clutch. She is elegant and graceful, always managing to keep her plumage in pristine condition.

Spooky, a peculiar hen from the light clutch, is small and has had various physical problems. The middle toe on her left foot was crooked until she was about twelve weeks old, at which time it straightened itself out. The slowest turkey to develop, she still has a rather downy head but has also become very healthy. Because of handling when she was injured or sick, she does not like to be touched, although if I ignore her, she will now come and sit close to me. I can stroke her only if my hand approaches very slowly.

In addition to Starker and Rosey there are only two other males, one of whom is very personable, Stretch; the other, a little shy, Turkey Boy. Normal sex ratios in wild turkeys are about 50 percent males and 50 percent females, according to Lovett Williams. The disparity in these turkeys' numbers is due simply to bad luck with disease and predators, which randomly involved more males than females.

Of the ten surviving females, I can easily distinguish almost all of them, but I do confuse two or three from the light clutch, as they are very similar in appearance. As the turkeys mature, distinctions become easier to make; appearance and personality become more developed and individual.

Since the time we began spending all of our days wandering and exploring away from the pen and the area of the cabin, I have recognized that something remarkable was occurring in our communication. At first it was difficult to interpret what was happening between us, but as time progressed I began to understand a little of what I now believe to be nothing less than extraordinary.

Wild turkeys are, at least superficially, a bit of a avian analogy for humans. We share certain "specific" attributes that have enabled this experiment to be more successful than I could have imagined. For example: Because the wild turkey is an extremely large bird, our sizes are not overwhelmingly disparate; we live principally on the ground; we are bipedal—our gait and stride are similar, making my movements across the land coordinated and undisturbing to the group; and we are social animals with extensive vocabularies. Wild turkeys in no way resemble little people, but these similarities have enabled me, as much as I am capable, to enter into their world and their experience without being a distraction to them.

These wild turkeys quite naturally think of me as their parent. As such, I observe that they expect me to conform to a very specific role, which they as young wild turkeys know and anticipate. They expect certain behaviors from me in filling the parental niche. In anticipation of these, they provide a sort of vacuum of expectation for me. When my behavior conforms to their expectation, their behavior is involved with all of the interesting and busy activity of a young wild turkey. Because I am the only thing in their environment that they can totally trust, predict, and thus afford to ignore, I become in a sense invisible to them. As long as I am doing the correct thing, as they perceive it, they need only concern themselves with maintaining a safe proximity and being attentive to any instruction I might offer. They are then free to involve themselves with more vital concerns like hunting for food and being watchful of predators. If, however, out of ignorance or thoughtlessness, I should deviate from my anticipated role, the young turkeys immediately cease their normal behavior and display a confusion that is characterized not by fear, but rather by an insatiable curiosity regarding my inappropriate behavior. They will forgo any activity they are involved with and obsess over my indiscretion until it is corrected. Only then will they proceed with normal behavior. In a very few weeks the young turkeys, in that way, taught me how this process is supposed to work; by a trial-and-error system I have generally learned most of what is expected of me. As a result, our behavior becomes synchronized somehow; something just clicks, and we become, it seems to me at times, like a single organism.

Some days when we set out to forage, I can feel that we are not in sync. Perhaps because we have not been together for some hours, there exists a kind of distance within our unspoken communication. Sometimes we find a secluded spot to sit and rest together, and then suddenly something happens—a sort of recollection of who we are occurs, and something links up—it is like an awakening. An enthusiasm wells up as we seem to remember our purpose, and we begin to work together.

I have been trying to articulate in my own mind, all summer, this phenomenon and the actual mechanics involved. I am experiencing a type of intimate communication unlike any that I have ever had. I cannot photograph this phenomenon, and it is difficult to write about, yet it is obvious that something remarkable is occurring.

I feel a little like an anthropologist who, after attempting to be an impartial observer of an exotic culture, finds himself instead becoming acculturated and confused about his own social identity. I haven't started eating grasshoppers yet, but the smooth green ones, I notice, are beginning to look very attractive.

The odds of a wild turkey reaching maturity are small. Approximately 50 percent of all nests are destroyed or abandoned. Among the surviving nests, some eggs will be infertile. Of the young turkeys who hatch, 70 percent will not last two weeks, and the number of survivors will continue to be diminished. The attrition rate of wild turkeys who have survived into maturity can be 70 percent per year. Wild turkeys are heavily selected by predators, and therefore could be classified as a prey species. Prey species typically compensate for this pressure by producing large numbers of offspring.

I have always imagined that, as a result of the mortality rate in young wild turkeys, enormous selective pressure must be operating to perfect the species. This experiment has demonstrated to me that the wild turkey that survives to adulthood in the fall is not merely a wise turkey or a clever turkey, nor is he necessarily a more adaptable or resilient turkey. Any poult that survives to maturity is primarily a lucky turkey. Selective pressures are possibly more important in the mature birds, with sheer numbers ensuring that a few will live to become exposed to these mechanisms. I would suggest that survival in young wild turkeys is primarily capricious. By no means are the fittest necessarily surviving into adulthood. It is probably only later in life that the wild turkey has the luxury of competing honestly in the selective survival game.

When I see an adult wild turkey now in his natural habitat, I have a new appreciation for the sheer phenomenon of his existence. It is very difficult to become a wild turkey.

August 31, Saturday

With thunderstorms on the horizon, we are hesitant to leave home, but by midmorning we decide to try for an outing. The temperature is pleasant, with a nice breeze resulting from the nearby storms.

I have been putting out cracked corn for several years now in an area approximately a quarter mile north of the pen. Various species of birds and mammals visit the feeding area regularly, including mourning doves, ground doves, quail, resident wild turkeys, various songbirds and crows, cotton rats, raccoons, foxes, deer, and coyotes. By night, screech owls are drawn to the area and prey on various species of mice including *Peromyscus nuttalli*, the arboreal golden mouse.

This morning as we approach the clearing there are eight or ten crows already on the ground eating. The turkeys immediately see the

crows and start running for the feeding area. As the crows begin to fly, the turkeys likewise take flight in pursuit. As a crow alights on an over-hanging limb, a turkey flies to that spot and chases him from the limb. The turkeys are very vocal, with tails spread wide in aggressive postures. The crows are likewise noisy as they express their insult with the turkeys. This behavior continues until all the crows are banished. Only then do the turkeys fly down and resume normal behavior.

The turkeys have always expressed a particular interest in crows. Perhaps they view them as competitors, or perhaps they just find them annoying. I am looking forward to observing this relationship as it develops.

We relax in the hammock for several hours and encounter pileated woodpeckers, chickadees, a hooded warbler, and a resident wild turkey who I can't see but hear yelp periodically. A hawk, possibly a Cooper's, flies past us at high speed and causes a stir among the turkeys.

September 1, Sunday

A cool autumn day in North Florida, it is 89 degrees with humidity below 75 percent. Although it seems as though we have come very far in almost four months, the time has slipped away, as long, hot days

have become weeks and the weeks months. It feels
like a short time has passed since the turkeys were
small and downy. They appear now as grown
wild turkeys, and I think I have grown as
well. We are fewer now, but that, I suppose, is the unending condition of the
wild turkey. Although our survival rate
is better than that of turkeys in the
wild, our losses seem great. With
our recent loss of the little hen
to the dog, I can see at a glance
that we are diminished. We are
fifteen now, if I include myself.

There is a dryness and a
movement to the air that
suggests fall is on the
way. Fall flowers
are beginning to
show, with sul-
phur and gulf
fritillary butterflies
dancing everywhere about
the old field. We wander down
Bert's Branch exploring some feeder creeks
originating in a large bay area that is a part of
Wren Nest and discover a game trail that will
take us out to the old field.

September 2, Monday

Although warm, the air is rather dry and of a quality
that must have its origin in a dryer, cooler latitude. It
promises that fall will eventually overtake the oppression of the summer, and that the tropics must surrender their suffocating grip, banished once again to lurk temporarily in some more equatorial domain.

A bit of the third world, with many of its environmental, social, and economic characteristics, has been deposited against the extremities of the Carolina Piedmont, it seems, in a geographic and environmental coalescence wherein the yellow poplar cohabits with the epiphytic orchid and the bromeliad. This is a land that does not know quite what to be and is in an eternal struggle for ecological identity. I have lived in the mountains of northern Wyoming and never suffered so much from the cold as in North Florida. I have been to tropical jungles, and I will put the summer heat and humidity of this country and the ferocity of its biting and bloodsucking insects up against any. In spite of all this, the area has a certain charm that some people come to love. Environmentally, it has had much to recommend it, although now these attributes exist primarily in vestigial remnants due to poor and greedy land management practiced by some large landowners, timber companies, and the national forests.

In Washington, D.C., terms like bayhead, titi swamp, gum pond, pine flatwood, and pine barren do not bring to mind something rare and beautiful. (The latter term is a misnomer, as there is nothing barren about a pine barren.) The immeasurable destruction that has occurred in these southern forests, which even in my lifetime stretched like a green ocean, has all but gone unnoticed. Unsuitable for farming, and with no particular desirability as recreational real estate, this land has suffered the misfortune of landing in the hands of large pulpwood holdings and the national government. Neither has been a good steward, and the rape that has occurred in the last thirty years is staggering. Trying to perceive the coastal pine flatwoods by observing a few hundred acres of remnant here and there is like trying to observe the ocean in a bucket of seawater. This great forest was an environmental phenomenon on a geological scale. For the most part this vast ecosystem is already gone, replaced by the sad agricultural process that is euphemistically referred to by business and government as "reforestation."

The planted slash pine—a voracious botanical cancer that only a mindless bureaucracy could propagate—incorporates all of the attributes that would cause a sawyer to declare a log worthless. These inferior trees will never grow to make a wood that can be used as lumber—they are useful only as pulp.

The real heartbreak of this practice lies in the absolute, irretrievable destruction that occurs to a complicated and fragile ecosystem. The poorly drained coastal flatwoods are not at all flat but exist as an elaborate mosaic of differing plant and animal communities that are dependent on slight variations in elevation. A mere six inches can, in many cases, account for vast differences in soil type, pH, and moisture. Further, two nearby habitats sharing the same relative elevation but otherwise isolated from one another can have subtle differences in soil makeup and hydrology that will account for completely different plant and animal communities. Often, these communities exist within an extremely narrow range of conditions. Anyone who has ever tried to transplant one of the unusual carnivorous plants or associated terrestrial orchids in these areas has learned how rigid their requirements are. Although they can be made to survive for some time, it is very difficult to provide an artificial environment in which they will flourish. Clear-cutting and so-called reforestation in the longleaf pine flatwoods ecosystem create a sterile monoculture and constitute an environmental holocaust that rivals the parking lot and the strip mine.

These native forests are resilient and generous. When their fundamental integrity is left intact, they will thrive on the rejuvenating effects of selective timber harvest and produce a significant sustainable yield. Slash pine "reforestation" is in fact the worst form of agriculture and involves completely denuding the environment, turning under the fragile soil, and corrugating the land with huge plows. Previously pristine North Florida rivers now run milky with sediment and nutrients, causing thick mats of algae to cover the otherwise clean beds of sand, gravel, and native aquatic plants. A seemingly infinite variety of habitat types is obliterated and washed away, the land forever reduced to its lowest common denominator. Even our national wildlife refuges have fallen prey to this foolish, destructive practice, and it would be charitable to say that these policies are the result merely of incompetent management.

The bugle of a bull elk in a high mountain basin, the haunting voice of a screech owl on a moonlit night, the song of a white-throated sparrow on a cold winter's morning, or the resounding call of a wild turkey gobbler in early spring—there are a certain few sounds in nature that seem to symbolize true wilderness. A gentle north wind moving through a remote forest of mature longleaf pine on a clear winter's day is one of those voices that stirs something deep inside of us. The grandest organ in the greatest cathedral is but a moan in the darkness by comparison.

There is a breath of fresh air, and we are grateful. The turkeys are very happy about the change in seasons and start the day with an impressive flight out to the middle of the lower field.

The dry air allows us to browse heavily and well into the day. The heat eventually returns, but the humidity remains low; the air continues to flow in the hammock. Invigorated, we change locations frequently, keeping our resting periods much shorter than normal—the turkeys continually explore and forage.

Aggressive behaviors are more common as a result of the weather, and several times during the day we have sessions of sparring punctuated by an occasional serious fight.

We find our first ripe wild persimmon.

September 3, Tuesday

Before going to town this evening, I manage to spend several hours foraging with the turkeys. The weather is again pleasant, and the turkeys are active and frisky. Very young wild turkeys are much too serious and cautious to engage in any activity that resembles play, but as they grow in size and begin to mature, they allow themselves a little latitude and show certain exuberant behaviors that resemble play—spontaneous, short, flight-assisted jumps, ducking and dodging as if some imaginary adversary exists, and chasing other birds and even snakes that attempt to flee. As the turkeys become larger than their predators of youth, they can relax more in their environment and even display a little arrogance. It is good to see. We no longer have to just take it, we can now dish it out a little.

We spend some very interesting hours exploring along Bert's Branch. Taking our newly discovered game trail, we pass between two springheads and their runs. The trees along the creeks are relatively large and include yellow poplar, tupelo, swamp chestnut oak, and magnolia, and these are surrounded by thick bay swamp. The bay swamp apparently feeds the seepage springs that contribute to Bert's Branch. The thick, dark green understory of the bay swamp bordering the hammock, coupled with the drop of the terrain into the spring runs and branch, is somewhat reminiscent of mountainous areas to our north. The saprophytic orchid called coralroot (*Corallorhiza wisteriana*) grows abundantly here on the damp slopes.

Upon arriving at the branch, the turkeys become very active as I sit and try to record their interaction. Two males get into a dispute that is rather violent and seems to last a long time. They both appear exhausted afterward.

We work our way carefully up the run of the branch and eventually find a spot on a downed live oak to relax as the day begins to warm.

It could appear to someone reading these field notes that I am continually stumbling along through this study with pen and notebook always in hand and cameras swinging and clanging around my neck. But in reality, I spend a relatively small portion of my time involved in these activities and, in fact, cannot find enough time to write about all that I would like. Finding snatches of time throughout the day, I jot down ideas and observations in a sort of shorthand of desperation that I hope will remind me of something I can expand on when it is more appropriate. (Like stars in a restaurant review, more than three bloody smudges on a page means mosquitoes were particularly bad that day.) Usually in the evening, I spend a couple of hours retrieving and reorganizing my thoughts while they are still fresh in my mind.

Unfortunately, time does not permit me to comment on each interesting event and experience during the day. Many more rattlesnake encounters occur, for example, than I can possibly write about; in fact, we may see as many as four large individuals in a single outing. We regularly encounter resident wild turkeys—often several occurrences in any one day—but they too are routine and often do not warrant comment. Our days are filled with a great diversity of experiences.

The majority of our time is spent gradually moving through the woods and fields. In order to be effective, I must move quietly and with some degree of grace. I must be inconspicuous, I must be safe, and I must be observant, both for the interesting activity of the flock as a whole, and for fourteen autonomous individuals who are constantly involved with all manner of interesting things. Some of these things are shared with the group, but others are not and so may go unnoticed. Frequently, I realize in frustration that encounters and events are occurring around me that are being missed. It is impossible to keep track of everyone and at the same time avoid falling over downed logs, thick palmettos, and large rattlesnakes. It is a constant challenge. Most of the time, it is totally inappropriate for me to do anything but be a silent pair of eyes.

An attendant discomfort is a part of this study. Ignoring the fact that I never get enough sleep, I typically stay wet all day. We march out in the early morning in a heavy dew, and the land is generally soaked from constant summer rainfall, so I remain damp, at least from the waist down, most of the time. In addition, the temperature is always high and the humidity is rarely below 90 percent. Evaporation does not occur under such conditions, and I am often soaked all day with perspiration. Multiple species of bloodsucking insects are with us at all times. The turkeys become distracted if I eat, and so with the exception of an occasional apple eaten on the move, I simply go without food. Ironically, the observation of life must be the ultimate distraction from reality. And so, mercifully, I do not normally think about biting flies, gnats, mosquitoes, ticks, and 95-degree heat and try remembering to worry, if I must, about heavy-bodied snakes and lightning strikes.

A certain repetition and monotony are an unavoidable part of our daily routine. We are out at sunrise, we wander about all day and eat things, and then we go home. In this sense, our days are always the same. But for me, there is a richness of experience that frequently borders on the overwhelming. When coupled with all the stressful conditions mentioned above, my mind, my body, and my senses are often in a state of near overload.

Further, I am subject to the ongoing insistence and presumption by these birds that I must be an integral part of their overall experience. With continuous reinforcement from fourteen strong-willed individuals—a subtle but unrelenting coercion that amounts to a form of indoctrination by association—it seems I have been gently molded into sharing a particular point of view. My will has gradually been overcome by the sheer weight of so much expectation.

These wild turkeys also have the disquieting ability to see past my eyes. This ability is a natural part of their behavior and communication, which I observe occurring within the group every day and for which I have absolutely no understanding. They reach within me, and at times I am convinced there is nothing about me of any significance that they do not know. It brings new meaning to the term "peer pressure."

Although I couldn't be having more fun, perhaps I have become a little worn down by the overall rigor of this experiment ("bewilderment" in its truest sense). Or maybe an adaptive change has occurred within and I am simply walking a path of less resistance. But, as the summer progresses, I find myself at last surrendering entirely to the moment and mindlessly allowing this experience to pass through me unimpeded by my attitudes and opinions. In spite of the verbal nature of this journal, I spend more and more time in a state characterized by a lack of any language-based thought process. All day I am inundated with a nonverbal form of communication that further reinforces this. Initially, I would find myself in this state of mind and try to resist, thinking it was contrary to my intent in this study—I should remain unattached, merely attempting to document what is unfolding around me. Interestingly, when my mind attempts to take control of the moment, I find that I am jolted back into my critical, analytical perspective. I am then no longer a participant, only a somewhat confused, disoriented, and disappointed spectator. A fragile bridge collapses, leaving me behind with my empty and seemingly irrelevant words.

At first, this subtle phenomenon—this lapse of normal consciousness—occurred only on occasion and for short periods. It was like driving an automobile and suddenly realizing you cannot remember being at the wheel for some unknown period of time. Gradually though, as the summer has progressed, I have unconsciously allowed myself to maintain this perspective for longer periods, until now I am sure I remain comfortably immersed in this state for perhaps hours at a time. Without a single word or thought or judgment I am transported into another world of experience, and at times I am overcome with the distinct realization that I am sharing a singular experience with these wild creatures. I feel as though I am seeing the world through their eyes, as though I am witness to their vision of the world.

And theirs is a vast world, where boundaries become indistinct, margins are vague, and edges, borders, and identities become obscurely woven into an elaborate tapestry of interaction and interconnection. Here, each thread is held in place solely by the grace and virtue of its orientation to all the others. It is a world where entities dissolve and exist as indivisible connections within an intricate network of fundamental relationships.

This journey is stirring me to rethink many of my attitudes and presumptions about the complexity and profoundly subtle nature of the experience within other species. I wonder about the possible universe of experience that has been unfolding around me, of which I remain unaware. I say I know the fox, but what I know is that she is a mysterious little soul who wonders why I can't keep up.

As we slowly work our way home in the early afternoon, a pygmy rattlesnake reminds us to be watchful.

Approaching the lower area of the old field, we run into a small covey of quail, which react to the turkeys by giving their two-syllable alarm call and moving briskly away. The turkeys appear amused or excited by the quail and begin chasing them about. Quail scatter around through the thick broom grass and young pines, eventually flushing in twos and threes. This aggressive interaction inspires the turkeys. They become animated—seemingly playful—jumping, ducking, and dodging back and forth making imaginary fighting gestures. The turkeys are becoming very cocky in their old age.

It rains very hard in the afternoon.

September 4, Wednesday

We leave the roost at first light. Browsing through the lower end of the field, we see that the crows are about and feeding in the field. Becoming very excited, the turkeys scatter in every direction as they fly out after individual crows. The crows are outraged and refuse to surrender the area. Wild turkeys become widely dispersed in large treetops throughout the eastern margin of the field and the adjacent hammock. It is a noisy and disagreeable business, with loud sharp turkey noise and crows screaming all about. Everyone eventually reaches a standoff and all flight seems to end, so Sweet Pea, who will have no part of such behavior, and I both begin calling from the field. Turkeys, scattered over a ten-acre area, begin flying in from all around. The birds seem very proud of themselves.

There is a tractor operating in a fallow cornfield bordering the east side of Bert's Branch, a quarter mile away. I imagine that the solitude of the branch will be temporarily disrupted by noise and choose to stay to the far west side of the old field. We silently browse the scrubby thickets as the tractor putts and clatters in the distance.

Arriving at the northern end of the old field around midmorning, we work our way along the national forest border and enter a stand of thick, relatively young longleaf pines. The trees in this area average ten to twelve inches in diameter. Limby, straight, and tall, they have closed in a canopy that, in consort with a thick bed of pine straw, has excluded almost all other vegetation. Consequently, it is pleasantly open, with only an occasional clump of wax myrtle, palmetto, or deer berry. The air is cooler here, and the turkeys have always found it to be an agreeable place in which to engage in leisurely wild turkey activities.

Entering the pine thicket a few minutes before the turkeys, I attempt to get a start on my apple before they arrive. The turkeys follow slowly and move across the area in anticipation of some relaxation.

I become involved in my own affairs, principally trying to keep my apple from a couple of turkeys who heard me crunching and came running. The others, who have worked their way past me twenty-five yards to my left, suddenly get into what appears to be a violent fight. The two turkeys who are with me run to join the action. I see it as a photo opportunity, grab the video camera, and start jockeying for position. While fumbling with lens covers and switches, I notice three turkeys running from the fight, which has become very noisy by now, and the others all set out in pursuit. The exception is Sweet Pea, who leaves the fray and comes running to me. Suddenly, I realize what is happening—we have at last been confronted by some resident wild turkeys, and I have spoiled the whole thing by standing up and making my presence known. These turkeys, of course, think they are responsible for repelling the assault and pursue the supposed vanquished rivals until they catch up with them. Another fight ensues, which I can barely see but again sounds violent. The residents then continue their retreat while these turkeys gradually return to me. I videotape the strangers as they walk in a semicircle around us to the south, engaging in loud alarm putting and occasional assembly yelps. They apparently became separated during all the confusion.

I find a beautiful tail feather pulled out in the fight, and an old cut on one jake's face is reopened and bleeding. We all sit close together, quietly watching the strangers until they eventually wander off to the south.

If I had been paying attention, I possibly could have recorded some very interesting interaction. Sweet Pea sits next to me the entire time, nervously voicing disapproval at all of this unpleasantness. Sweet Pea is a lover, not a fighter.

The first false foxglove (*Agalinis purpurea*) is blooming in the old field, and there are acorns on the running oaks. Green acorns from laurel and water oaks are falling in the hammock. The turkeys may be heard continually clattering about as they mouth the acorns, but as yet they do not seem to be eating any except those that I break open.

Soon after the resident wild turkey encounter, I collect an empty box turtle shell and we gradually forage in the direction of home. The day heats up in the early afternoon, and we long for the cool recesses of the branch, but the tractor and the heat are relentless.

September 5, Thursday

Again this morning there is a pleasantness in the air, and in spite of the relatively warm temperature we are very glad to be where we are. A continuous breeze blows from the east, rapidly pushing low, damp, billowing clouds past us, causing the sun to alternately appear and disappear like the opening and closing of some great shutter. The old field, as usual, proves bountiful for the turkeys, and they are constantly engaged in the business of getting food. My tendency is to move rapidly through the field, always looking either directly underfoot or far ahead in anticipation of the next interesting experience. Every moment I am reminded by these wild turkeys of this foolish human predisposition—looking constantly from my own feet into a future that, by its own definition, will never exist, a perpetual condition whereby we live our lives, alternately, from blinders to blindness. The turkeys will not buy into it, and if I want to go stumbling ahead into some egocentric cosmic abstraction, they will let me. For this reason I try to let them lead the way as much as possible, and they teach me about wild turkey speed and wild turkey time.

Wild turkey speed is that speed beyond which an organism becomes stupid on a scale proportional to the relative increase. In other words, stupidity is directly proportional to the square of one's velocity. For this reason it is very difficult for me to travel at wild turkey speed. Every day is a new lesson in this discipline. Wild turkey speed allows one to utilize consciousness and sensory awareness to minimize one's expenditure of energy. A wild turkey always proceeds as if he were in the perfect place at the perfect time. All his needs may be satisfied here in this moment. These opportunities are merely waiting to be recognized—a constant condition of sustenance through inquiry and discovery. I find that it is difficult for me to avoid being goal oriented in our outings, betraying the moment for some abstraction up ahead. An absurd and ironic result of this is that the rattlesnake, which serves as a perfect metaphor, is peacefully waiting to be understood and instead winds up underfoot. There is no profit in this, and these wild turkeys constantly remind me to do better. Their experience, which I believe to be vastly richer than my own, affords them an awareness and evolutionary maturity that is far superior. I have made this natural world my devoted life's work, but they remind me that I am a clumsy pilgrim in a realm that can never truly be my own.

Wild turkey time is more difficult to explain. It seems to have something to do with a resolution of the time it takes for a grasshopper to fly and land, and the time it takes to get from the Cretaceous to the Holocene. Wild turkeys exist on a vast continuum like continents and mountain ranges but only in this moment like the wind on your face. And, as any turkey hunter knows, they exist only as a probability, a tendency to occur in a certain place at a certain time. They behave at once like a particle and like a wave, and even a physicist would call them unpredictable. A wild turkey suddenly is there like a gnat in your eye or he is an apparition that gives you occasion to doubt your senses. In either case, he can be very hard to get to know.

By midday it is very warm, and we head to a cool location on Bert's Branch. I immediately settle in to work on my field notes while the turkeys relax in a thicket of shrubs behind me. Sweet Pea climbs in my lap, of course, and goes sound asleep. Our disappearance is accomplished, and so we noon. Nooning involves the passage of wild turkey time, and so it is very hard to gauge. It is surely either a few moments or a few hours, and I remain suspended in it.

Eventually, I realize that no one has wandered past in a long time, nor have I heard any activity in the thicket. I sound a soft yelp, which is normally answered with a small chorus of turkey noise. I hear no reply, so I whistle a faint lost call, which also receives no answer except from Sweet Pea. I call louder, and still I hear no reply. Sweet Pea becomes concerned about everyone's whereabouts and begins to scan the area behind us with her sharp eyes and ears. I can tell that she sees or hears nothing as she slowly begins to walk in the direction of the thicket. As she moves into the brushy area behind us, I stand up and follow. This is very odd. There are no turkeys anywhere to be seen. Sweet Pea becomes noticeably upset as she realizes that we have been left alone. Nothing like this has ever happened before. We wander south along the east side of the hammock, occasionally lost calling and scanning the woods ahead. Sweet Pea appears almost frantic as she hurriedly weaves through vegetation and calls for her brothers and sisters.

Approximately one-quarter of a mile down the hammock, we begin to see turkeys up ahead. As we arrive, seeing the majority standing out in the edge of the field that was mowed by the tractor the day before, they chatter their customary greetings. Sweet Pea is noticeably relieved, but I am very concerned about this new development and don't understand what has just occurred. I join the flock, give an assembly call, and head back into the hammock. To my very disturbed surprise, they yelp and chatter acknowledgment but do not follow. Instead, they continue east out into the field following an old hedgerow and fence line that leads perpendicularly away from the hammock and in the direction of a graded national forest road two hundred yards away. By moving in front of the flock and walking back through them toward the hammock, calling, I attempt to turn them. They refuse to follow and seem intent on following the hedgerow. They have never failed to follow me before, and they are wandering in the worst possible direction. There is a farm nearby and frequent traffic on this road, and they will surely be seen. I am beginning to feel frantic myself as they refuse me again and again. They seem to have suddenly made a break with me but in a location that could be dangerous for them. We are very far from home, and I do not want it to occur like this.

I try moving ahead of them once again, but this time as if I am leading them away from the hammock. They move slowly as they explore this interesting new territory. Gradually, I begin to veer to the north away from the hedgerow into some rough field above the recently mowed area to the south. They follow me to the north, but when I gradually move our course in the direction of the hammock to the west, they refuse. And now we head directly toward a small farm complete with yard dogs.

Eventually, some of the turkeys begin to follow me in an oblique angle that heads indirectly back to the hammock. Others still want to move farther out in the field, and so we remain spread out, making it all the more difficult to communicate.

Finally, we hit the old overgrown roadbed that fords the northern part of Bert's Branch. The turkeys are still ambivalent about heading in this direction, but enough of the group follows to entice the others to follow also. An eternity seems to pass before we reach the ford on Bert's Branch. Thirsty and overheated, the turkeys are relieved to be near water as it is the hottest time of the day.

But again the turkeys refuse to follow me, as they stall on the creek. Some wander into the hammock, while others appear to want to go back to the east. I stand helplessly on the west side of the hammock in plain view and lost call as the turkeys decide what they want to do.

I watch the turkeys, feeling hurt and somewhat betrayed by them, while they very comfortably mind their own business and ignore mine. At least we are back within the borders of our home range, where there are no fences or dogs. I feel sick from the stress of the last couple of hours. Although I knew that something like this could occur any day now, I am stunned by the abruptness of it all.

I realize suddenly that the turkeys are assembled on my side of the branch and are slowly foraging in my direction. To my eventual surprise and relief, they all join me on the edge of the old field and casually follow me down the old roadbed as they have so many times before. I head as directly as possible toward home, feeling exhausted, and having had enough excitement for one day. I know things are different now, and I must arrange for the turkeys to be on their own.

We quietly drift toward home along the sandy trail of the roadbed. With some dread, I have anticipated today's disturbing event, and, in fact, I have for some time now recognized the turkeys' developing confidence and independence. This is exactly what should be occurring now, and yet, curiously, I am very upset, actually in pain. Some closed place deep within, where I must have stored ancient disappointments and betrayals, has been knocked ajar this afternoon. Old, strangely familiar sorrows grab at me as I slowly walk along—wounds that I thought were long since healed. In spite of all that we have shared, I am surprised at the depths into which I have allowed these birds passage. My mind is clear and calm, but a powerful visceral attachment has been strained. How odd . . . human beings are such strange creatures.

Part IV

September 10, Tuesday

The turkeys are now free to come and go as they please. I spend as much time as possible with them, alternately sitting with them and going inside the cabin. Occasionally, we go out for short foraging walks in the lower part of the field. They seem to be making the transition gracefully, with a minimum of confusion. They are extremely capable and seem to know exactly what to do with themselves.

I sit with them in the evenings until they fly up on the roost in the trees surrounding the pen. I do this not for their benefit but for mine—to see them independent yet choosing to remain in the vicinity. Likewise, I join them in the morning as they fly down, again not because they need me, but because I need the continuity. We are developing a new and different relationship, and I want to remain close enough to the turkeys that I may serve their needs as they change and develop. Recognizing that their needs may best be served by a lack of interference from me, I want to be sensitive to what is going on with them. Ideally, I would enjoy having a relationship in which they live their lives independent of me yet allow me to join in on occasion as if I belong.

One of the hens has received a deep cut on the top of her head, and I am keeping her in the pen. She has a slight infection, and I want to be able to treat her. I am also keeping a couple of others penned up, so that she will not get upset when left alone. Periodically, I let one of them out and replace it with another who volunteers to enter the pen.

The turkeys in the pen serve to keep the larger group close, as they do not want to be separated. I think this will help all of us in the transition.

October 15, Tuesday

We slowly browse the lower areas of the old field. The temperature is high, so we move directly from one shady area to the next. After entering a large clump of wax myrtles, I sit down to observe the turkeys in their activities. They immediately start putting, and we find that we have joined a black racer that has also chosen the cool cover of the wax myrtles for an afternoon refuge. His repose has been completely disrupted, but the turkeys show only obligatory interest and eventually ignore the unhappy snake.

The wax myrtles have grown up under the protection of several medium-sized loblolly pines. The myrtle thicket in turn provides suitable moisture and shade to promote the growth of small water oaks, a seedling holly, and a perimeter thicket of blackberries. We exhaust the browsing potential of the myrtles after a very few minutes, much to the relief of the black racer.

Stooping to clear the low cover of vegetation within the thicket, I quietly move across a thick moist bed of dead wax myrtle leaves and pine straw. Suddenly, I feel my foot touch something hard that immediately gives way with a crunch. I bend down on one knee and begin gently digging through the pine straw and leaf litter.

A damp, yellow, mealy substance is smeared in the mulch, and first I think that it is the meat of some boletus mushroom, but I cannot account for the sharp crunching sensation that I felt under my foot. Uncovering more leaf mulch, I discover that I have stepped on a large egg. I dread the smell of hydrogen sulfide that must by now be well imparted to my fingers. I carefully smell my fingers, but there is only a musty, earthy smell. The egg is obviously that of a wild turkey and no doubt has remained protected and covered in this thicket since spring. It has desiccated to the consistency of a hard-boiled egg but has not rotted. I am reminded of the four eggs in clutch #2 that did not develop and, even in the heat of the incubator, did not become rotten but rather achieved a similar state. I examine the surrounding leaf litter, wondering if I may have inadvertently located an abandoned nest, but find no other eggs. Nevertheless, it may be a nest site and this an infertile egg, left behind and never discovered by predators or scavengers.

Looking at the large, powerful birds who surround me now, I cannot reconcile the change that has occurred since I was caring for an incubator full of eggs. Despite having been with them every day of their lives, it appears to me that something must have occurred while I was not looking. Perhaps I was following the flight of a distant hawk or tracing the route of a frog through the glistening water of the branch, but something has happened of which I have not been a part. My notes are incomplete. Nothing that I have seen or heard in these few months can begin to explain the development standing before me now. My experience with these wild birds has been a phenomenon of an explosive and yet subtle nature. This present manifestation is not reducible by me to a body of observations that would allow me to explain any of it. My perception is too slow to fully embrace what has occurred, but a realization has been imposed on me by these elegant birds. As we leave the confines of my language and culture, these graceful creatures become in every way my superiors. More alert, sensitive, and aware, they are vastly more conscious than I. They are in many ways, in fact, simply more intelligent. Theirs is an intricate aptitude, a clear distillation of purpose and design that is beyond my ability to comprehend.

As human beings, we are born ignorant and helpless, empty vessels that must be filled by tedious years of experience and study. We start from nothing and over the years must totally reinvent ourselves again and again. These wild creatures are heir to tens of millions of years of an accumulated wisdom, handed down directly from one to the next, defying mortality. Just as the warm flame of their being has never grown cold, the incandescence that sustained their ancestors for perhaps twenty million years similarly preserves the bright sentient flame of their ancient conscious transaction with life.

This is the transcendent message contained within this broken egg that has been catapulted from some remote antiquity into this moment. Like most inquiries, this study has left me with more questions than answers. I am not disappointed, however, but rather a little relieved as I realize that a mystery I have grown to love will remain intact. I will be content to wonder.

EPILOGUE

It has been almost two years since I assumed responsibility for two clutches of orphaned wild turkey eggs. During this period, there has been scarcely a day that I have not been involved, directly or indirectly, in their lives. In this time, not one moment has passed or one interaction transpired that I have not been gratefully aware of the extraordinary nature of our relationship.

As of February of their first year, the entire flock of fourteen wild turkeys remained together in the immediate vicinity of Wren Nest, although by that time they had completed their polarization into two distinct groups—gobblers and hens. The males remained well defined by their fraternity, while the hens gradually became more independent and solitary.

Knowing that the spring breeding and nesting season was nearing, I had two plans: Since radio-telemetry studies have shown that juvenile hens leave their home range and pioneer a new territory, often many miles away, for their first nesting (probably serving to prevent inbreeding); and, since the spring gobbler hunting season was also at hand, I was determined to see that the males at least might survive their first spring season, and further wanted to experiment and see if the wild turkey hen's biological predisposition to find a new home range for nesting might terminate after the onset of egg laying. By keeping one gobbler in the pen at all times and at least two hens, and rotating this occupancy every day or two, I found that all of the gobblers and most of the hens tended to stay within the immediate area. It was my intention to rotate the males in the pen until the five-week hunting season ended, and continue rotating the hens until eggs began to appear in the pen.

This process seemed to work beautifully. As the turkeys never learned to dislike their pen, finding new volunteers to relieve their siblings every day or so was a simple matter. This close proximity during the breeding season allowed me the opportunity to observe the complicated and well-defined social order that exists among sibling wild turkey gobblers.

Within the group consisting of four males, Rosey, the larger gobbler from the light clutch, had always been and remained the undisputed dominant bird. When fierce aggressive behavior occurred on rare occasions, it invariably involved disputes between the other three males: Stretch, Turkey Boy, and Starker.

Rosey was granted unchallenged access to the hens and assumed the role of a typical adult gobbler. Accompanying his spring breeding behavior, consisting of continuous strutting, drumming, and well-articulated gobbling, was the development of secondary sexual characteristics including the extreme permanent swelling of the caruncles and the soft fleshy tissue of the head. The cartilage over the eyes, within a few weeks, became thick and enlarged. The snood grew to a length of four or five inches, and a heavy breast sponge, a large protective deposition of fatty tissue, developed. With the exception of spur length and first-basic plumage, he was to my eye indistinguishable from a mature two-year-old gobbler. The other gobblers retained in every way their juvenile behavior and appearance, with little or no strutting, no extraordinary development of the caruncles or the tissues of the head, and no breast sponge; and none but Rosey ever attempted to gobble.

Since many wild turkey behaviors associated with sexuality, including strutting and mounting behavior, occur within the first few days or weeks of life, I am assuming that these are unrelated to the release of testosterone or other hormones. It appears obvious to me therefore that unrestricted breeding activity has promoted the functioning of Rosey's endocrine system somewhat prematurely and encouraged the development of the more obvious secondary sexual characteristics seen in adult gobblers.

Within the fraternal order, a tenuous and delicate balance of power appears to be maintained through a system of constant acknowledgment and reinforcement of status. Through an ongoing series of subtle signals, denoting the affirmation of dominance and submission, sibling wild turkey gobblers manage to remain together and, at least on the surface, present a picture of relative harmony. But when this subtle aggressive/submissive interaction is interfered with, tension quickly builds to the point of intolerance, and serious fighting inevitably occurs.

The signals to which I refer include certain stares and the avoidance of these "evil eye" stares; turning away and avoiding direct frontal confrontation; lowering the head and surrendering one's immediate space; and ultimately assuming a submissive sitting posture with neck outstretched low as far away as possible from the individual expressing dominance. These gestures vary from exaggerated and obvious on occasion to discreet and abbreviated most of the time.

It appears that order, and indeed membership, within the group must be verified if not reestablished many times each day. I have found that if for some reason a male is separated from the group for as long as a day, or in particular for a night, it is only with great and often violent difficulty that he is allowed readmission. At one point in the spring, Starker left with some resident wild hens and was on an apparent walkabout for two days. Upon his return, he was persecuted and denied admission to the group for several days. All three of the other males participated in attacks.

Interestingly, even though I have been the parent to these wild turkeys and so presumably occupied the role of the hen to some degree, at no time was there any confusion about, or interest in, my sexuality by any of the males—an exclusion for which I am grateful. Consequently, I was permitted to be an impartial or at least uninvolved observer, although, as I will explain later, this would eventually change.

Although most of the hens remained close to Wren Nest, some could not resist the strong urge to strike out on their own. We began getting reports from neighbors concerning interesting visitations by friendly wild turkeys. Claudia received a phone call from one of her students, Kacie Tartt, reporting an unusually tame wild turkey feeding in her yard. We agreed to come take a look and so received directions to the home. The residence was located on an inholding within the national forest. Upon arrival, I recognized Samara, who allowed me to gently pick her up and place her in the back of my covered pickup truck. She calmly walked around in the back of the truck as we drove the five miles back home. Arriving home, I opened the back of the truck, and she gracefully hopped out and immediately joined some of her sisters. She remained in the area for a couple of days and then chose to venture away once again. I am not sure if I ever saw Samara again.

On occasion, Rosey would reside within the pen for a day or two, and as breeding time was occurring among many receptive hens, the other three males also occasionally had the opportunity to mate. Since the majority of hens were from the light clutch and the other three males were from the dark, this seemed like an opportunity to avoid some of the inbreeding that would have inevitably occurred. Rosey, however, thought poorly of my reasoning.

By the end of April, hens were beginning to disappear and eggs were appearing in the pen. Sweet Pea and Rosita were the last hens to be housed in the pen, and both were beginning to lay an egg every day or so. By this time I had collected over two dozen eggs within the pen, laid by various hens (which I refrigerated for later specimen preservation). After these two hens had each laid several eggs randomly about the pen, I released them in hopes that they would begin nesting nearby. My experiment appeared to work; both Sweet Pea and Rosita began nesting in the area.

After these two hens had completed laying, they began to sit and would only appear briefly once or twice a day while on "recess." This would often occur in mid- to late afternoon in the heat of the day, although occasionally one would appear in the late morning. Most of the other hens seemed to move off to the north, up into the national forest, perhaps to find remote nesting sites.

The males, for a time, remained attached to the immediate area of Wren Nest, and so I would spend the majority of my available time with them and was allowed to accompany them on foraging expeditions. With the exception of Starker who appeared to have a brief tryst with a small group of resident wild turkey hens, I observed no interaction between these gobblers and the wild residents during this period. Although I was never allowed to observe directly any of Starker's interaction with the resident wild hens, I was able on two occasions to sit and listen, from a distance of fifty yards or so, to their vocal exchanges. Even though the hens were not attended by a mature gobbler, I judged their vocalizations to be expressions of annoyance with him, although this interpretation may be incorrect, as he was allowed to accompany them for two days. I suspect he was relieved of duty by some cranky, battle-weary old veteran. Starker, who generally managed to maintain his plumage in better repair than some of the other males, was in some disarray when he finally returned.

My relationship with the turkeys continued to be very close and almost, one could say, loving. Although Rosey's responsibilities as dominant gobbler caused him to be somewhat preoccupied and aloof, the other males retained their fondness for my proximity and for physical contact.

No matter where we were, whenever I would sit on the ground, against a tree, with legs outstretched, Starker would stand or sit in my lap and preen. Frequently, the other males would gradually join him, and occasionally there would be fifty or more pounds of wild turkeys sleeping and preening on my legs.

Stretch had the peculiar habit of walking directly up in front of me, if I was sitting, adjusting his wings carefully on his back, standing square footed with his head lowered down onto his "shoulders," and closing his eyes while I held and gently stroked him. He would remain in that posture for five or ten minutes and seemed to desire that attention every day or two.

By following Sweet Pea and Rosita as they wandered back to their nests after a recess, I was able to determine the approximate location of each of their nest sites. The hens began incubation during the same week, but after the second week Rosita showed up early one morning very nervous and with half of her tail missing. I walked to her nest site, less than a quarter of a mile from the cabin, and found that she had narrowly escaped capture by some large predator. I assume it was a bobcat or a coyote, although I cannot be positive. Broken pieces of eggs were scattered about, as well as a double handful of feathers from Rosita's side, rump, and tail. She might have another opportunity to produce offspring, since it is common for wild turkeys to nest a second or even a third time in a single season if things do not go well on their first attempt.

I have to admit that I had some half-baked notions about a hen showing up with a newly hatched brood in time to avail myself once again of a modified imprinting opportunity, which would allow me to accompany a brooding hen with young poults unafraid of my presence. In other words, to begin this whole process again but from a completely different point of view. It seemed no more implausible than the rest of this strange experience.

Sweet Pea continued showing up around the cabin during her recesses, although some days she would not appear. When she arrived looking for an easy meal, she would be relaxed and friendly and occasionally would allow time for sitting or standing in my lap preening.

After several weeks of incubation, Sweet Pea stopped coming for her daily recesses, and I began to suspect that her brood had hatched. I imagined her secretly guarding them in some solitary thicket, in the cover of the old field, carefully watching the red-shouldered hawks circling overhead and cautiously skirting the locations where she knew an old rattlesnake might be lurking.

A week or so passed with no sign of Sweet Pea and her brood. I decided to try to locate her nest site. I knew only the general vicinity of the nest, which was located in an area where we harvested gallberries on the upper west side of the old field. I wandered around for a time recalling various experiences we had in this solitary area. Just as I entered the location where the turkeys and I had our first face-to-face encounter with a deer, I noticed a broken eggshell. A few yards farther I saw more shells and then, to my dismay, feathers.

I sit on the ground in the sun with the dried and tattered remains of Sweet Pea lying in my lap. A piece of a wing, chewed and gnawed, a few of her beautiful tail feathers, a clump of feathers from her breast still attached to a piece of dried and crinkled skin, a handful of long graceful tail coverts. The surrounding field and woods blur and swirl as I cannot contain my sadness. I sit limp contemplating how I possibly could have allowed my life to become so entwined with the lives of these fragile creatures whose existence is so tenuous, whose business it is to die in such great numbers, and why it should be my business to care this much. I try to imagine my world without Sweet Pea, and the prospect seems barren. I have thoughtlessly entered into an arrangement with these birds that I must have assumed would last forever. I am shocked that her extreme competency could be overcome so quickly. I wonder if it may have been in her gentle nature to hesitate one instant too long in protecting her nest. I feel a deep sadness for the occupants of these crushed and broken eggs. Sweet Pea must have in her way treasured them. Could they have come to know her voice from within the warm confines of the egg? Were their eyes developed enough to enjoy the vague illumination that must have diffused their small world at times while their mother was away? Did it cause them to anticipate in some way the comfort of the warm sun?

I feel a sense of loss for all the unique and interesting personalities that would have been, all the intelligence and grace that they would have brought into the world and the joy that they would have expressed. How much richer, it seems, the world would have been with them.

Perhaps somewhere now there is a den of bright-eyed coyote pups that are more prosperous or a sleepy pair of bobcat kittens resting more comfortably in the base of a hollow tree. This is the unforgiving game we have chosen to play, and these are the rules.

One Saturday morning in late May, only a few days after finding Sweet Pea, the gobblers assembled in the hammock near the cabin and were watching me. I tried to ignore them, for I knew they wanted me to join them on an adventure, but I was very busy. Gradually, they moved off to the north without me and were gone. For a week or so there was only Rosita, who would visit for an hour or two each day. She seemed restless and distracted, and soon she too ventured away, and for the first time in over a year I was without wild turkeys in my life.

Although I was happy for their independence and even relieved to have my own independence returned to me, I felt empty and a little disoriented. This was the phenomenon of the "empty nest" in its most literal sense. I found myself rising early and being drawn up into the old field toward the national forest. Visiting areas where I knew wild turkeys might be found, I would sit and wait for a familiar face, but no one came. Walking the length of the old roadbed, I would check for any activity that might be recorded in the sandy areas of the ruts. There was none. Even the resident wild turkeys were nowhere to be found. In fact, the entire area appeared to have become devoid of life, and the old field seemed once again a worn-out old stand of weeds and second-growth timber. I had become accustomed to a privileged entry into a hidden realm that was afforded solely by my proximity to these wild turkeys. For a short time my humanity was forgiven, and I was allowed access to a world that had finally closed its doors to me.

The coach whip no longer had time for my observations and would not confront me with his brave eyes. The cardinals that had been so curious and so casual these few months now appeared to be uninterested in my company, even frightened, and would no longer sit and preen nearby. The fierce red-shouldered hawks displayed little interest in my comings and goings and would not alight close by to examine me. Even the crows moved away silently as I approached and refused to interact. I walked carefully along the margin of the hammock and cautiously regarded the old rotten log pile, but the rattlesnakes would not reveal themselves. I felt lonely. I longed for the richness of experience, the dedication of purpose, and the perfect companionship. I feared that no one else could ever come to know me so well, so clearly—how transparent their honesty made me, how unimpeachable was our devotion to each other.

Weeks passed with only an occasional report of a sighting by neighbors or people in the area—usually a lone hen who would pass by or visit briefly but no sightings of any of the males.

While I was running errands in Tallahassee one day in mid-June, Claudia managed to reach me in the afternoon and reported that one of the males had returned; she knew only that it was neither Rosey nor Starker.

I rushed to Wren Nest immediately and discovered that it was Turkey Boy, who had returned home alone. This male, whose personality had been eclipsed by the others, had seemed less aggressive in his need for direct interaction with me, always close but always on the periphery of things. He was a little enigmatic. For whatever reason, he chose to be with us at Wren Nest for the following year and proved to be one of the great joys of my life.

Later in June, I received interesting news from Chris Parkinson, a friend who owns and lives on a twenty-acre parcel within the national forest, several miles to the northeast. She notified me that two wild turkey hens had taken up residence on and around her undeveloped land, with six or seven poults in their company. The hens would readily lead their brood into her yard and actually forage at times in the shrubbery adjacent to the house. She stated that so long as she remained inside, they appeared indifferent to her, her house, and her surroundings, but they would run or fly if she ventured outside. Judging by her description, the poults were around eight to ten weeks old. They remained nearby for the following month but gradually came with less regularity, and by August she stopped seeing them.

Throughout the summer, Turkey Boy maintained an interesting balance between his world and mine, venturing off on occasion with a few resident wild turkeys but always returning after a day or two. Perhaps, thousands of years ago, it was an odd personality in some individual wild turkey that made their eventual domestication possible. There appeared to be something in his particular nature that caused him ultimately to prefer our company to that of his own kind. He eventually seemed to desire only my company on his daily foraging walks and outings. I considered any day not spent in some sort of adventure with Turkey Boy a great opportunity missed for me and a distinct disappointment for him.

With Turkey Boy as my liaison, I once again gained entry into his world and his vision. We made frequent and intense study of the creeks and hammocks, finding secret and hidden recesses that we had overlooked in the past. On any day we could quickly locate some fat and sullen old rattlesnake secretly preparing for the coming fall and winter.

At times in the thick damp gallberry, wild azalea, and possum haw, with me on hands and knees, we would spend hours making new discoveries, finding new things, and communing with the damp inhabitants such as salamanders—mole, slimy, marbled, and red-eft—and tree frogs—squirrel, green, gray, pinewoods, and spring peeper. It is a wild turkey's business to know the whereabouts of these things, although as Turkey Boy matured, they became less significant to him as food and more as things of interest and curiosity. Often he would locate and observe various snakes and be overcome with the need to snatch them from their hiding places and toss them into the light of day. Although no such disrespect was ever shown the rattlesnake or the surly cottonmouth, the rat snake, the ring-necked, and the racer did not escape some obligatory torment.

Even though Turkey Boy definitely had his own set of priorities, he was always very attentive to my activities and interests and seemed to display great respect for my limited powers of observation. Anytime my attention would become focused on one thing or another, he would invariably acknowledge this by coming, often a considerable distance, to investigate. Somehow the leaves that I was browsing through were always more interesting than his own. And I could do one amazing and magical thing that he could not—I could roll over a rotten log!

This is a dark, moist realm, blanketed by the lush green fern moss and adorned with brilliant markers of extraordinary hue and value. Upon the moldy remains of some decaying wooden torso are the vermillion hygrophorus, the yellow witches butter, and the viscid violet cort, vivid markers and signposts meant to turn the head and gain the eye of something wild, a semaphore of sorts to those aboriginal creatures that know the language of color, that know the lay of the land. But beneath this shroud of color lies entombed not the dull slumber of death but rather a concealed world of fertility and life. Such a wonder and mystery—such intimacy and privacy exposed—such bounty. First, a shrew, then a salamander, a ground skink, a narrow-mouthed frog, then a spadefoot toad, a nest of white-footed mice, and fat white grubs—secret things to ponder, terra incognita, food for wild turkeys,

food for wild thoughts. Carefully returning a log to its previous approximate position, we would proceed to the next, our appetite for the obscure insatiable.

I marveled every day at the extraordinary nature of our attachment. A bond that we could not acknowledge, for it was clear that Turkey Boy had no need to question, to test, or to doubt—no more than he had occasion to doubt the sky over his head or the ground under his feet. It could not be verified with a certain contact made eye to eye, nor, of course, could we express these things verbally. Only when we would turn away could I feel something pull inside, or when I would see him in the distance, intent on his own business, could I feel something physical tugging at me from within. We were each a flame, one for the other, to which like moths we were both drawn. At times I could see him standing in the distance, searching for me when we had become separated, or could hear him cautiously calling for me across a thicket when I could not be seen. I could sense that neither of us was ever truly comfortable in the absence of the other.

Turkey Boy gradually established a routine around Wren Nest. Roosting was done in the hammock, west of the cabin, either in a certain large sweet bay tree over the roof or in a very large native slash pine that towers over the forest below. Many mornings at first light a great thump on the roof would serve as my wake-up call. Most mornings I was able to join him, at least on a short tour around the lower part of the old field. Each time I joined him, he greeted me with his happy dance, a brief joyful display of ducking and dodging, with wings outstretched and a frisky shake of the head like a dog with water in his ears. Occasionally, he would jump at me and touch me lightly with his feet. His anticipation and enthusiasm made it difficult for me to disappoint him.

During the day, while I worked in my studio, Turkey Boy would alternately browse the surrounding hammock, visit the bird feeding station, and sit, dozing and preening, but always in sight of me through two large plate-glass windows on the back corner of the cabin. He quickly learned, after only two frightening attempts, that it was impractical to try to join me through the glass.

If and when I had to leave Wren Nest, Turkey Boy would always insist on running along after me. As a result the only way I could get away was to drive slowly several hundred yards up into the old field with a wild turkey following and then, as he joined me, speed back in the other direction as fast as I could go, leaving him far behind. It always made me feel very bad, but fortunately he would not attempt to follow me past the gate once I was out of sight. In this way, I clocked Turkey Boy over one hundred times, and his maximum speed on foot appeared to be sixteen miles per hour—any faster and it would cause him to spontaneously take flight, pass me like a rocket, and stand blocking the trail fifty yards ahead. The speed at which wild turkeys can run has often been exaggerated.

Further, Turkey Boy would always have to accompany me on my daily run, my middle-aged mileage regimen being never less than two, never more than five. I run on an approximate half-mile oval trail around the lower part of the old field. On a cool day Turkey Boy could maintain the pace, following immediately behind, for about one-third to one-half mile. (I run at a rate of about eight miles per hour.) After this distance he would quickly fall behind and would then accompany me cleverly by running in smaller and smaller concentric circles until eventually he would be in the center of the field browsing around in a fifty-foot circle. When I completed my run and began walking to cool down, he would then join up by "leading" me one hundred yards or so and meet me on the trail.

I did discover, however, that wild turkeys, like people, respond to training and conditioning, and eventually Turkey Boy improved his distance to one mile, although his maximum speed appeared to remain constant at about sixteen miles per hour. I judged that he could maintain his top speed for no more than a quarter of a mile.

It was obvious that it was not the location of Wren Nest that held Turkey Boy nearby but rather the company. Invariably, if Claudia or I were not at Wren Nest, he would be drawn north toward the national forest. Many times when I returned home, he would not be in the area. Hiking up to the national forest border, I would often find him loitering about in the area where resident wild turkeys frequently moved down from the north. Occasionally, I would suddenly see him standing, perhaps seventy-five yards away, as still as a statue. I would stop still, to make sure whom I was observing, and we would cautiously scrutinize each other. Eventually, I would make a sound that he would recognize, and I would see him relax, shake off, and then begin casually walking toward me. On more than one occasion I had difficulty locating him and walked long distances yelping and lost calling. Eventually looking to my rear, I would realize that he had been calmly browsing along a few yards behind perhaps the entire time—probably wondering who I was looking for.

One day I looked up and at thirty yards foolishly spoke in my natural voice to a horrified resident wild gobbler: "There you are, Turkey Boy!"

One afternoon in late August, while walking up to the feeding area north of the cabin with a bucket of corn, I suddenly looked up and the bait site was full of wild turkeys. Everyone was motionless at about thirty-five yards.

Two of the hens from the light clutch were standing in the middle of a crowd of startled poults. I counted twelve or thirteen before the group started running for cover. The two hens remained in the feeding area a few seconds and then started running after their poults. I whistled a lost call and both stopped, momentarily, and then continued after their brood.

This was very late in the summer for young poults, and so I suspected they could have been the result of a second nesting attempt. But they were large with first-basic tail feathers, probably ten weeks or older. Old enough to have a good chance for survival. I hoped one of the hens was Rosita, but I will never know for sure. That was the only time I saw them.

From spring throughout the summer, Turkey Boy systematically molted away his first-basic plumage, which was ready for retirement, and received his first installment of fully mature plumage. Because of the nutritional advantages that these wild turkeys received, I am certain that they have grown more rapidly and eventually to a larger size than their resident counterparts. By sixteen months, Turkey Boy had become large and powerful, standing taller than my waist. His very full beard was around eight or nine inches, his spurs were both over three-quarters of an inch, and his weight was between sixteen and seventeen pounds. Not yet in his prime, he was already as big as any two-year-old gobbler I have observed.

Turkey Boy was casual and friendly around the yard and cabin, and I knew better than to try to insulate him from things. He was too clever for that. Any food or drink that I chose to carry outside had to be shared. If it was food for me, it must be, without question, food for wild turkeys. He shared my morning coffee, at noon he relished my turkey sandwich, and in the evening he delighted in my cabernet. Wine is but liquid berries to a wild turkey. When my glass was emptied, there would be a small deposit of gray sand in the bottom from Turkey Boy's gritty mouth. Claudia is a devoted gardener, and Turkey Boy would spend hours assisting her in digging, planting, and weeding. He was a proficient thinner of greens, occasionally to Claudia's chagrin. But she adored Turkey Boy, and, ultimately, he could do no wrong. He would call softly to her, and she would answer in a low voice—"Birdie."

I knew that the minute he left the relative safety of the immediate area, he was all business. A wild turkey is by definition always a target, and he thankfully was infinitely more aware of that than I. Our association was never a compromise to his inherent wildness.

One afternoon, while I was away in town, Turkey Boy was browsing along with Claudia, up on the east side of the old field adjacent to the thick hammock, but not far from the cabin. It was a clear, sunny, and warm afternoon in late November. Claudia was quietly walking thirty or so yards ahead of Turkey Boy as he calmly foraged among the tall grasses. Suddenly there was a great commotion; Claudia spun around to the powerful flapping of wings and a vocal cry that she

described as the definition of desperation. Claudia yelled spontaneously and began to run toward the uproar. She saw a terrified wild turkey running from the grasp of a large predator. She could not see well from her position and could only say it was probably either a coyote or a bobcat, which disappeared instantly in the thick wall of the hammock.

When I returned home that night, I was shown the location of the attack. We collected a grocery bag full of feathers from Turkey Boy's rear, including three tail feathers and many beautiful tail coverts. The ground was grassy and dry, so I could not locate a good track. Turkey Boy was uninjured in the attack, and in eight weeks all of the missing feathers had been replaced, but thereafter he regarded that location with a quiet suspicion.

The resident wild turkeys in this area are seasonal migrants. From spring, throughout the summer, into early fall, we usually have a few nesting hens and juveniles and very rarely an adult gobbler. By November things begin to change. Perhaps their movement coincides with the onset of hunting season, or maybe it has to do with the lack of a good food source here or the availability of better food elsewhere; in any case, they all leave the area, and from late November until late spring we will not see a single turkey—not one track.

As winter began to set in, Turkey Boy remained and no longer had the opportunity to interact with other wild turkeys. Gradually, he shifted all his remaining social attention toward me and Claudia. For weeks and months he remained close, never disappearing into the forest for an overnighter. He grew even more fixated on me and our companionship. The cool days of winter allowed us to range and explore long distances, and for a time it was wonderful. As winter began to round the corner toward spring, January saw a beautiful, mature, wild turkey gobbler coming into his own. Turkey Boy began to change.

With Turkey Boy having no innate social concept of a parent who would continue to interact after the first few months of life, I wondered what sort of place I occupied in his wild turkey mind. Was there room in there for a genderless companion? What did I represent to him socially?

One day I was outside the cabin on my knees pulling up some thick gallberry and sweet pepper bush, expanding my bird feeding station. Turkey Boy enjoyed this type of activity and would always be in attendance, grabbing worms, grubs, tree frogs, and such as they became exposed to him. Suddenly I realized that he was acting more interested in me than usual as I thrashed around pulling and tugging on the tangled roots. He obviously was becoming excited by this strenuous activity, and so I stopped to try to find out what was going on. He stood very close and nervously looked straight into my eyes in a way that made me feel uncomfortable. I spoke to him calmly and reached out. He pecked violently at the back of my hand, sending a dash of blood across the skin. Not understanding what was occurring and having been inadvertently hurt many times by these birds, I reached out again, and once again he attacked violently, drawing blood. In a reflex action I thumped him across the breast with the back of my hand, more of a shove than a slap, and said, "Hey, what are you doing!" It was for him a revelation. All his switches flipped—all his lights came on—and through what I gathered to be some sort of transference, he completed my evolution from parent to companion to adversarial brother. Turkey Boy had discovered that his mission in life was to fight. I started toward the front door of the cabin, but he repeatedly blocked my path and confronted me with angry fighting gestures. I dodged around him and made my way inside, and, as I moved through the cabin, he would follow me from window to window, glowing with vivid violet, livid red, and lurid purple. Strutting and drumming at me, he was furious, antagonistic, and loving it. As I ran cold water across my injury, I realized my feelings hurt more than my bleeding hand.

I wondered what had occurred, what it meant, and how I should deal with it. I thought if I stayed out of sight, he might cool down and forget, but for him there was nothing else in life. I was his obsession. There was obviously nothing that would please him so much as a fight to the finish with me. Turkey Boy was powerful; he was constructed for this. By now he was pushing eighteen pounds, his spurs were well over an inch long and sharp. Gestures that I had become very familiar with were now being directed at me, and I have to admit that he was frightening. He gave me the evil stare; he trembled with contained and focused rage. He seemed like some sinister cross between an eighteen-pound gamecock and a chain saw.

I thought of a plan. Perhaps if we could confirm that he was dominant over me, we could establish a new relationship based on his superiority. With this in mind, I ran from the house out into the grassy field with the turkey monster in pursuit. I threw myself on the ground face down and covered my head with my arms and hands. The angry bird marched around, alternately jumping at me and furiously pecking and tugging on my clothes. He pulled the cap from my head and for a time paraded around me with the cap in his bill, shaking it up and down, as if proudly displaying some gruesome trophy that he had severed from my head. His display was so exaggerated that for a moment I had to laugh, but soon he dropped the cap and again focused his rage on me. My face hidden, I endured several minutes of agony as he repeatedly attacked my head and hands. He alternately stabbed and gouged me with his powerful beak. My hands and ears began to bleed as I waited for him to release his anger and declare his dominance. Perhaps I was unable to send the appropriate signals, but I soon realized that the well of Turkey Boy's wrath was bottomless. I could stand no more. I jumped to my feet and sprinted to the cabin, the angry and victorious beast fast on my trail.

I had a serious problem on my hands. I tried ignoring him, avoiding eye contact, turning away—all the avoidance tactics I had observed the other males employing to avert serious confrontation, but I could not convey the message correctly. Nothing worked.

When I left the cabin in the afternoon for my daily run, it was open season on me. Being much too clever to just pursue me around the field exhausting himself, he would cut across the field, lie in wait, and attack me as I ran by. Wild turkeys fight face to face, in the air, spurring, pecking, and slapping each other with powerful, bruising blows from their wings. This all occurs at about eye level to a human and so can be very dangerous.

Eventually, one day, desperate after having been spurred badly in the back, I realized this had to stop. Furiously, I broke off a single long-leaf pine bough four feet long and turned to defend myself. Thinking that the cushioning effect of the long green pine needles would prevent any serious injury from occurring, I hoped perhaps I could intimidate him into, at least, respecting me enough to leave me alone.

Turkey Boy jumped and spurred. Dodging powerful wing blows, I swung back. With each attack I swung with all my strength, and our blows intersected with a loud slap and clatter. At one point I lost my footing as I swung and went down. Turkey Boy was immediately all over me. Regaining my footing, I swung hard again, and this time the end of the pine bough caught him square on the head and neck and sent him reeling backward.

Suddenly, with the vivid color disappearing from his head, he turned without looking back and ran in a straight line due north for as far as I could see. I had sadly prevailed, and I felt that he had surrendered all. I would probably never see him again.

Returning to the cabin bleeding, battered, dirty, and exhausted, I was sickened by what had occurred. I felt like a child who had just had a terrible fight with his best friend, and in winning I had ultimately lost so much.

When I awoke the following morning, to my astonishment there was Turkey Boy, refreshed, glowing with the colors of battle, and ready for round two. I had already decided that there would never be a round two. This business is never finished with a wild turkey; I knew that.

I had read that human-imprinted mature gobblers become aggressive toward humans, and so I had feared all along that this was a possibility. Turkey Boy, however, never became in any way hostile toward anyone but me. He was gentle and loving with Claudia and protective of her when I was near. He continued to be friendly and cordial with all guests and strangers, male and female. It did appear, however, that, if only by coincidence, he had managed to assign gender to Claudia and me correctly. Additionally, it became obvious that he still wanted only to be with me and remained attached to me in every way as

before, only now I had become a player, a real participant in his life—
a brother.

I eventually learned through various avoidance tactics how to partially divert Turkey Boy's aggression. I became adept at reassigning his
hostility toward other interests and found that by entering unknown
territory on long walks his attention would be, for a time, directed
away from our fraternal order of conflict and onto other things. Occasionally, I would jog up through the field from the cabin with Turkey
Boy aggressively following. But as we left the immediate territory surrounding Wren Nest, his anger would subside or be displaced by more
important concerns. At times we would relate for hours the way we
had in the past, exploring, gathering food, or just relaxing in the sun
and preening. But invariably as we came within sight of Wren Nest,
and in particular if Claudia were near, he would become angry, and I
would have to enter the cabin. I avoided confrontation at all costs.

An area veterinarian who works with wildlife suggested experi-
menting with the drug Depo-provera. A powerful hormone used for
birth control in some European countries, Depo-provera is legal only
for veterinary applications in the United States and is frequently used
to control aggression in male birds, particularly parrots. It is risky and
in some cases causes liver and kidney damage if used too often. After
the initial injection, behavioral changes begin to occur gradually in a
few days, and one treatment can be effective for up to a month or two.
The vet knew nothing of the effect on turkeys but gave me an exper-
imental dose formulated for a body weight of eighteen pounds.

That evening I stood outside, and when Turkey Boy attacked me,
I grabbed him by the neck, holding the syringe in my mouth, wrestled
him down, and quickly injected the drug into his large breast muscle.
It was like pouring gasoline on a fire and it took days for his anger over
being restrained to subside. For the next four weeks there was
absolutely no change in his behavior.

A few weeks later, on a rainy Saturday morning in early April, as
Claudia was walking up in the field, by some lucky coincidence she
happened to see Turkey Boy standing beneath a thick young pine. He

was deathly sick, barely able to stand. We had spent time with him the night before, and he seemed to be in perfect condition. Claudia led me to him, and I very gradually managed to have him follow me to the pen. I immediately filled the waterer with diluted Terramycin, but Turkey Boy was near death and would neither eat nor drink. He walked to the back corner of the pen and lay down.

New neighbors had recently arrived nearby and had stocked their place with almost every domestic fowl known. I am sure that wild birds were alternately foraging in their barnyard and visiting my feeding station. Turkey Boy could have been exposed to anything, including black head disease.

Curiously, Turkey Boy, despite the recent presence of domestic turkeys nearby, had never shown the slightest interest in them or their crude vocalizations.

Monday morning found me at the veterinarian's office, obtaining large doses of the antibiotic Enrofloxacin to be delivered by injection twice a day for ten days. Initial injections of vitamins B-12 and A were also prescribed. Unless these treatments acted immediately, I saw no way that Turkey Boy would survive more than a day or two.

I entered the pen with three syringes for his initial treatment and was amazed to find that when I grabbed Turkey Boy, he fought with considerable strength; it was only after an enormous struggle that I managed to complete all three injections. I couldn't let Claudia participate, for I knew that if he lived, he would never forgive her for being associated with all this sickness, fear, restraint, and pain. I now worried that the trauma of the treatments might steal his little remaining strength and kill him.

The next morning, he saw me coming with the syringe and started to panic, trying to fly and hitting the fence. Only with great difficulty did I capture and restrain him and eventually give the injection. It was clear that neither of us could take any more of this abuse, and so I decided that the treatment was as destructive as the disease. I determined to stop the antibiotic and let Turkey Boy live or die in relative peace.

For nearly three weeks, he lay in the back corner of the pen, head down, as close to death as a bird can be. Blood rose to the surface of his head, partially in response to the fever and partially in response to the gnats, which he had not the strength or the will to ward off. His head turned black.

On two occasions, I considered killing him rather than watch him waste away so pitifully. He lost half his body weight and was terribly dehydrated. Barely able to peck, he would manage to get down only a few fresh greens that Claudia would hold for him. But I remembered that these wild turkeys had always done well when allowed to make their own decisions regarding critical matters, and so I decided to let Turkey Boy deal with his death in his own way.

Nearly three weeks into his ordeal, I awoke one morning to find Turkey Boy in the usual place, sitting on the ground with his head down, but the floor of the pen had been completely overturned. He had been scratching for food with some apparent ambition. Three days later, he was up and walking around. I started him on high-protein commercial poultry feed, which he had not had since he was a poult, and he ate with great enthusiasm. The scabs and discoloration of his head had begun to disappear and were being replaced with a healthy powder blue, white, and light pink. Once again, this remarkable bird, whose entire life had been so unlikely, appeared to have beaten the odds.

Two days later, still worried that he might be too weak to fly up to roost, or might even relapse, I opened the pen with a handful of fresh greens and coaxed him through the door. To my amazement, Turkey Boy showed a little nervousness around me but no aggression or hostility whatsoever. We went straight out into the field and found the nearest gopher tortoise burrow, and while I lay on the ground beside him, he comfortably, and with apparent joy, dusted and preened.

In the days and weeks that followed I feared that Turkey Boy's aggressive behavior might be rehabilitated along with his good health—but it was not. He quickly grew strong and again very healthy. He gained weight rapidly, but all hostility toward me was erased. Even in the company of Claudia and me together, he was again gentle and content. Perhaps the Depo-provera had some delayed residual effect, or perhaps his disease had moved his biological clock forward, past the breeding season, but he no longer gobbled in the mornings, he never strutted, and the vivid aggressive colors were absent from his head. Now, when we met, he would again do his happy dance, and I knew that our relationship had been restored.

I soon came to understand that things were not entirely the same in Turkey Boy's life, however. There had been a slight reordering of his priorities. Perhaps it was part of any wild turkey's development, part of his inevitable maturity, but I began to realize that our relationship was no longer central to his life. He began to be more independent and was beginning to look away. Resident wild turkeys were returning to the area, and perhaps he was simply remembering who he was. Gradually, he was drawn up into the forest.

Some weeks have passed since I last saw Turkey Boy and many months since I have seen any of the others. Every day I walk slowly up toward the forest along the old roadbed and look for signs; I see fox, coyote, two raccoons, several armadillos, a few crows collecting grit, beetle tracks, ant lions, a slender-bodied snake—probably a coach whip—but no wild turkeys. I know April is a busy time for them. Perhaps later there will be an opportunity for a brief encounter. I can feel them pulling me. Somehow I can still feel our attachment—some luminescent thread, a sort of articulation of the spirit—and I know in their own way I am still a part of their experience.

Perhaps one day a seasoned and wary old bird will answer and come to my call, and as he stands cautiously observing the odd lump that sits propped against the base of an old oak, there will be some peculiar element of familiarity that will cause him to remain for a moment longer. I might observe a crooked toe or a mandible that imperfectly occludes or receive a subtle message conveyed by some language that we both understand but cannot speak, and I could say: "I know you, old friend. I recognize you by your iridescence, your incandescence, your illumination—I recognize you by your loneliness—you must be my brother."

REFERENCES

Aldrich, J.W. 1967. *The Wild Turkey and Its Management*. (Washington, D.C.: The Wildlife Society.)

Austin, O.L. 1961. *Birds of the World*. (Toronto: Musson Book Co.)

Bickerton, D. 1990. *Language and Species*. (Chicago: University of Chicago Press.)

Brodkorb, P. 1960. "How Many Species of Birds Have Existed," *Gainesville Bulletin*, Florida State Museum 5:41–53.

Davis, H.E. 1949. *The American Wild Turkey*. (Georgetown, S.C.: Small Arms Technical Publishing Co.)

Fernald, M.L. 1950. *Gray's Manual of Botany, 8th ed.* (New York: American Book Co.)

Gleason, H.A. 1952. *The New Britton and Brown Illustrated Flora of the Northeastern United States and Adjacent Canada*, 3 vols. (New York: New York Botanical Garden Publishers.)

Godfrey, R.K. 1988. *Trees, Shrubs, and Woody Vines of Northern Florida and Adjacent Georgia and Alabama*. (Athens: University of Georgia Press.)

Godfrey, R.K., and Wooten, J.W. 1979. *Aquatic and Wetland Plants of Southeastern United States. Monocotyledons*. (Athens: University of Georgia Press.)

Godfrey, R.K., and Wooten, J.W. 1981. *Aquatic and Wetland Plants of Southeastern United States. Dicotyledons*. (Athens: University of Georgia Press.)

Healy, W.R.; Kimmel, R.O.; and Goetz, E.J. 1975. "Behavior of Human-Imprinted and Hand-Reared Wild Turkey Poults," *Proceedings of the Third National Wild Turkey Symposium*, The Wildlife Society, Texas Chapter, Austin.

Hitchcock, A.S. 1971. *Manual of the Grasses of the United States. Vols. I and II, 2nd ed.* (New York: Dover Publications.)

Leopold, A. 1933. *Game Management.* (New York: Charles Scribner's Sons.)

Leopold, A.S. 1943. "The Moults of Young Wild and Domestic Turkeys," *The Condor* 45, no. 4: 133–45.

Lorenz, K. 1952. *King Solomon's Ring.* (London: Methuen & Co.)

Lorenz, K. 1988. *Here Am I—Where Are You? The Behavior of the Graylag Goose.* (New York: Harcourt Brace & Co.)

Luer, C.A. 1972. *The Native Orchids of Florida.* (New York: New York Botanical Garden Publishers.)

Olsen, S.J. 1968. "Appendix: The Osteology of the Wild Turkey," *Fish, Amphibian and Reptile Remains from Archaeological Sites.* (Cambridge: Papers of the Peabody Museum of Archaeology and Ethnology.)

Ornstein, R. 1991. *The Evolution of Consciousness.* (New York: Prentice Hall Press.)

Radford, A.E.; Ahles, Harry E.; and Bell, C.R. 1964. *Manual of the Vascular Flora of the Carolinas.* (Chapel Hill: University of North Carolina Press.)

Rosenfield, I. 1992. *The Strange, Familiar and Forgotten—An Anatomy of Consciousness.* (New York: Alfred A. Knopf.)

Small, J.K. 1933. *Manual of the Southeastern Flora.* (Chapel Hill: University of North Carolina Press.)

Steadman, D.W. 1980. *A Review of the Osteology and Paleontology of Turkeys.* (Los Angeles: Contributions in Science, Natural History Museum of Los Angeles County.)

Stoddard, H.L., Sr. 1931. *The Bobwhite Quail, Its Habits, Preservation, and Increase.* (New York: Charles Scribner's Sons.)

Stoddard, H.L., Sr. 1963. *Maintenance and Increase of the Eastern Wild Turkey on Private Lands of the Coastal Plain of the Deep Southeast.* Tall Timbers Research Bulletin 3.

Tinbergen, N. 1989. *The Study of Instinct.* (Oxford, England: Clarendon Press.)

Vince, M.A. 1969. "Embryonic Communication, Respiration and Synchronization of Hatching," in R.A. Hinde, ed., *Bird Vocalizations,* pages 233–60. (New York: Cambridge University Press.)

Williams, L.E., Jr. 1981. *The Book of the Wild Turkey.* (Tulsa, Oklahoma: Winchester Press.)

Williams, L.E., Jr. 1991. *Managing Wild Turkeys in Florida.* (Gainesville: Real Turkeys Publishers.)

Williams, L.E., Jr., and Austin, David H. 1988. "Studies of the Wild Turkeys in Florida," *Technical Bulletin,* no. 10. (Gainesville: University of Florida Press.)

Wing, L.W. 1956. *Natural History of Birds.* (New York: Ronald Press.)